Beyond the Business Plan

# Beyond the Business Plan
## 10 Principles for New Venture Explorers

By
Simon Bridge
*Visiting Professor of Entrepreneurship, University of Ulster*

and

Cecilia Hegarty
*Director, PLATO EBR, N. Ireland and Ireland*

© Simon Bridge and Cecilia Hegarty 2013
Softcover reprint of the hardcover 1st edition 2013 978-1-137-33286-8

All rights reserved. No reproduction, copy or transmission of this publication may be made without written permission.

No portion of this publication may be reproduced, copied or transmitted save with written permission or in accordance with the provisions of the Copyright, Designs and Patents Act 1988, or under the terms of any licence permitting limited copying issued by the Copyright Licensing Agency, Saffron House, 6–10 Kirby Street, London EC1N 8TS.

Any person who does any unauthorized act in relation to this publication may be liable to criminal prosecution and civil claims for damages.

The authors have asserted their rights to be identified as the authors of this work in accordance with the Copyright, Designs and Patents Act 1988.

First published 2013 by
PALGRAVE MACMILLAN

Palgrave Macmillan in the UK is an imprint of Macmillan Publishers Limited, registered in England, company number 785998, of Houndmills, Basingstoke, Hampshire RG21 6XS.

Palgrave Macmillan in the US is a division of St Martin's Press LLC, 175 Fifth Avenue, New York, NY 10010.

Palgrave Macmillan is the global academic imprint of the above companies and has companies and representatives throughout the world.

Palgrave® and Macmillan® are registered trademarks in the United States, the United Kingdom, Europe and other countries.

ISBN 978-1-349-46194-3      ISBN 978-1-137-33287-5 (eBook)
DOI 10.1057/9781137332875

This book is printed on paper suitable for recycling and made from fully managed and sustained forest sources. Logging, pulping and manufacturing processes are expected to conform to the environmental regulations of the country of origin.

A catalogue record for this book is available from the British Library.

A catalog record for this book is available from the Library of Congress.

Typeset by MPS Limited, Chennai, India.

# Contents

*List of Case, Figures,
Illustrations and Tables*  ix
*Preface*  xiii
*Acknowledgments*  xvii

| Part I | Why Look Beyond the Business Plan? | 1 |
|---|---|---|
| 1 | The Purpose of This Book | 3 |
| 2 | Business Plans – Why Are They Advocated? | 13 |
| 3 | Are Business Plans Appropriate? | 27 |
| 4 | Business Plans Are Not the Only Option | 41 |
| 5 | Enterprise and Exploration | 51 |
| 6 | A Guide for Explorers? | 65 |
| Part II | The Ten Principles | 71 |
| 7 | The Starting Point: Understanding How to Explore | 73 |
| 8 | Principle 1 – An Enterprise Is a Means, Not an End | 81 |

| | | |
|---|---|---|
| 9 | Principle 2 – Don't Commit More than You Can Afford to Lose | 89 |
| 10 | Principle 3 – Start from Where You Are | 97 |
| 11 | Principle 4 – Carry Out Reality Checks and Make Appropriate Plans | 103 |
| 12 | Principle 5 – The Only Reliable Test Is a Real One | 109 |
| 13 | Principle 6 – Get Started and Get Some Momentum | 119 |
| 14 | Principle 7 – Accept Uncertainty | 131 |
| 15 | Principle 8 – Look for Opportunities | 141 |
| 16 | Principle 9 – Build and Use Social Capital | 147 |
| 17 | Principle 10 – Acquire the Relevant Skills | 159 |
| 18 | Following the Principles | 165 |
| **Part III** | **Seeking a Balanced Perspective** | **171** |
| 19 | Striking a Balance | 173 |
| 20 | Comparing Approaches | 179 |
| 21 | Some Reflections and Implications | 193 |
| 22 | Postscript – The Relevance of Exploring | 207 |

| | | |
|---|---|---|
| **Part IV** | **Further Information** | **215** |
| 23 | Behavioural Economics | 216 |
| | Causation and Effectuation | 217 |
| | Caution and Proceeding Cautiously | 221 |
| | Legal Structures | 223 |
| | New Venture Terminology | 226 |
| | Social Capital | 229 |
| | Social Enterprises | 242 |
| | Traits | 244 |
| | Additional Aspects | 248 |
| *Notes* | | 255 |
| *Index* | | 271 |

# List of Case, Figures, Illustrations and Tables

## Figures

| | | |
|---|---|---|
| 2.1 | Business start-up: The strategic planning process | 15 |
| 8.1 | Maslow's hierarchy of needs | 83 |
| 8.2 | What are an individual's goals? | 86 |

## Illustrations

| | | |
|---|---|---|
| 1.1 | Starting a small consultancy business | 3 |
| 1.2 | Examples of enterprising ventures | 6 |
| 1.3 | Enterprise terminology | 7 |
| 1.4 | Holywood Old School | 10 |
| 2.1 | Some advice for people starting businesses | 13 |
| 2.2 | Two parallel views on small businesses | 19 |
| 3.1 | Do business plans help new ventures? | 28 |
| 3.2 | Business plan scepticism | 31 |
| 3.3 | The limitations of market forecasting | 32 |
| 3.4 | The business plan as a start-up syllabus | 37 |
| 4.1 | *A Better Mousetrap* | 42 |
| 4.2 | *So what? who cares? why you?* | 42 |
| 4.3 | Lean Startup | 43 |
| 4.4 | Effectuation | 45 |
| 5.1 | Christopher Columbus: Explorer or entrepreneur? | 52 |

| | | |
|---|---|---|
| 5.2 | Explorers and maps | 57 |
| 5.3 | Clock or Cloud? Analysing something through its component parts | 61 |
| 7.1 | But which way is best for you? | 75 |
| 7.2 | Explorers often don't get it right the first time – but that isn't failure | 79 |
| 9.1 | The danger of trusting a business plan – and of putting too much at risk | 93 |
| 11.1 | Checking scientific theories | 104 |
| 11.2 | Holiday preparation | 105 |
| 11.3 | Some prior provision can be helpful for unforeseen eventualities | 107 |
| 12.1 | The coat question | 112 |
| 12.2 | Lean Startup | 113 |
| 12.3 | Exploring the market – for real | 116 |
| 13.1 | Early perseverance can pay off | 119 |
| 13.2 | Ready–fire–aim | 120 |
| 13.3 | The relevance of getting started and gaining momentum | 122 |
| 13.4 | When to reconnoitre and when to jump in? | 123 |
| 13.5 | The rock climbers' approach? | 125 |
| 13.6 | When prior reconnaissance may be a waste of time | 126 |
| 13.7 | An entrepreneur's view | 128 |
| 14.1 | Why there can't be route maps for new ventures | 135 |
| 16.1 | A social capital example: The importance of a supportive social circle | 151 |
| 16.2 | Finding a mentor | 153 |
| 17.1 | The 'Management Trinity' | 160 |
| 17.2 | Can you do it all yourself? | 162 |
| 18.1 | Beware of instinctive rationalisations | 167 |
| 21.1 | Summary of comparison | 197 |

| 22.1 | Creating unnecessary failure? | 209 |
| 23.1 | The principles of Effectuation | 219 |
| 23.2 | The importance of social 'rules' | 240 |

**Tables**

| 2.1 | The start-up strategic process | 16 |
| 2.2 | A business plan layout | 17 |
| 8.1 | Possible goals | 82 |
| 8.2 | Other ways to find resources | 84 |
| 8.3 | Possible reasons for launching a new venture | 87 |
| 10.1 | What makes a good idea? | 98 |
| 10.2 | Comparison of goal-focussed and mean-driven approaches | 100 |
| 11.1 | What to check | 106 |
| 14.1 | Different operating approaches for prediction, risk and uncertainty | 134 |
| 16.1 | Some of the benefits available from networks | 155 |
| 16.2 | Some 'rules of the road' for networking | 156 |
| 20.1 | Comparison of exploration-based and business-plan-based approaches | 188 |
| 20.2 | The advantages and disadvantages of exploration-based and business-plan-based approaches | 190 |

# Preface

As the introduction to Part I explains, this is a book for 'new venture explorers' – those people who want to find a good way to develop a new venture, which might be self-employment and/or a business of some form, but might be something else, such as a new club, society or project.

Anyone starting a new venture is likely to be doing it because they want to see what they can do themselves to achieve a goal, whether that is for their own benefit or to help others, instead of waiting for someone else to do something about it. However, people starting a new business or other enterprise are venturing into what is likely to be, at least for them, something new and uncertain. Such people are therefore explorers, trying to create new ventures to take them to where they want to go or to find something they want to have.

Therefore this book refers to such people as new venture explorers – both because that highlights the exploratory nature of what they are doing, even if they think they are trying to establish a new business, and because to attach the label 'business' to such ventures does lead many people then to think of them as embryonic big businesses and to apply big-business-based thinking to them much too early.

The aim of the book is to provide those new venture explorers with guidance relevant to their endeavours. Understanding how to venture – how to try a new initiative rather than just hitching a ride on an existing one – is potentially a very useful ability.

A few years ago it might have been assumed that any new economic venture would have been a business, and if this book had been written then it would probably have described itself as a business start-up guide. Further, it would have advocated a business plan, not simply as a key tool to use for starting a business, but as an essential requirement for such a venture. However, this book does not do that. Instead it maintains that a new venture does not necessarily have to be an embryonic business and that, even if a business is contemplated, a business plan is not necessarily the best tool to use. A new venture is inevitably something of a step into the unknown because it is a move into the future, and the future is not pre-ordained. It is a form of exploration – and for that a business plan is often not the best aid, and can even be counter-productive. That is now being recognised in some quarters but, nevertheless, business plans are still often advocated.

Therefore this book:

- challenges the assumption that a business plan is a universal tool for a new enterprise venture;
- suggests that new enterprise ventures are, and should be seen as, a form of exploration which may, or may not, lead to business;
- offers, therefore, a set of exploration-based principles as a relevant guide for any new enterprise venture; and

- suggests that business plans are a specialist tool only useful for particular situations within business and which can do more harm than good if used on other occasions.

The book presents this message in four sections:

Part I explains why business plans have become the advice of choice for many professional business advisers, trainers and/or funders who want to assist start-ups. But business plans are not the only way and there are other options for new ventures. In particular most new ventures have lot in common with exploration, so ten principles are suggested to guide new venture explorers.

Part II expands this exploration approach based on guidance from the ten principles. After reviewing the nature of exploration and its relevance to new ventures, each principle in turn is explained and its essence and application illustrated. This part then concludes with reflections on following the principles, which are designed to guide the explorer without being prescriptive.

Part III then seeks to provide a balanced overall perspective on the relevance of the exploration approach. Having, in the first two parts, criticised the business plan and highlighted the relevance of exploration, this part provides a comparison between the two approaches. It recognises that they are like two different tools, each of which can be useful for different tasks. So guidance is provided on when each might be most helpful, and the comparison concludes with reasons for suggesting that the exploration approach is often the better tool for new venture explorers.

Part IV is entitled 'Further Information' and it provides supplementary information on a number of factors or issues. In some cases these are mentioned earlier in the book, but in a situation where providing fuller information about them might interrupt the flow of the relevant chapter. In other cases the subject is not mentioned earlier, but some people might nevertheless have expected to see it – so it is outlined in this section together with reasons why it is not considered earlier.

The three main parts are thus different in both form and content in order to offer different perspectives relevant to the new venture explorer. Part I looks at the traditional advice and why it may not be very suitable. It is therefore intended to prepare new venture explorers to resist the sort of traditional guidance they are likely to be offered while also indicating what sort of help might be suitable. Part II then contains the book's core message, distilled as ten principles to present the advice that this book suggests is appropriate. After that, for those who want it, Part III provides a more balanced perspective. It considers the advantages and disadvantages of each main approach but indicates why, nevertheless, an exploration approach is likely to be the most suitable for the majority of new venture explorers. Thus, in order to make each part as self-contained as possible, there is some repetition of arguments and anecdotes, but the authors have endeavoured to keep this to a minimum.

# Acknowledgments

The authors are very grateful to Stiofan Daltun, Paul Graham and Aaron Taylor for permission to comment on and/or reproduce their work. They are also conscious of the many people who have encouraged them to explore these ideas about new venture creation and/or have made their own comments or suggestions, both directly and indirectly. Unfortunately they are too many and disparate to list here, but thanks are due for their contributions also.

# Part I
# Why Look Beyond the Business Plan?

> Key Learning Objectives
>
> From Part I the reader should learn that:
>
> - This book is for 'new venture explorers': people who want to explore the creation of a new enterprise in some form.
> - Business plans are often advised as an essential requirement for new ventures. In particular, business 'professionals', who tend to apply big business thinking, like business plans and often advocate them.
> - However, there is evidence that business plans do not help many new ventures and there is now considerable scepticism about them.
> - There are other guides for early stage ventures and an 'effectual' approach is often used by successful entrepreneurs.
> - An analogy with exploration suggests that new ventures are a form of exploration and that this is consistent with effectuation.
> - Maps and pre-prepared route instructions are unlikely to be available to guide new venture explorers. Instead, a set of guiding principles for exploration is suggested.

This is a book for new venture explorers – people who, instead of being content always to wait for other people to do things first, want to see what they can do themselves to create and/or develop something that they think would be helpful.

However, anyone starting a new venture, especially if they describe it as a new business, is likely to be advised that they need to prepare a business plan. That advice is often favoured by accountants, consultants and other business advisers, since businesses plans are often helpful to them. However, it is based on big business thinking, which is not necessarily appropriate for small businesses and in particular start-ups.

There are criticisms of the business plan and alternative guides are available. Among the other views considered is the concept of effectuation, which is also consistent with looking at new venture start-ups as a form of exploration. Therefore, based on effectuation and exploration, a set of exploration principles is suggested in this book as a guide for new venture start-ups.

Chapter 1 is about the purpose of this book. Chapter 2 then introduces business plans and analyses why they are advocated. Chapter 3 shows why business plans are not helpful for most new ventures and Chapter 4 then considers alternative guides, especially effectuation. Effectuation is consistent with seeing new ventures as a form of exploration, and this analogy is considered in Chapter 5. A set of principles based on it are suggested in Chapter 6 as a guide for new venture explorers.

# 1
# The Purpose of This Book

> **The Essence of This Chapter**
>
> - This is a book for 'new venture explorers': people who want to create a new enterprise.
>
> - New ventures can take a wide variety of forms.
>
> - Some of the terminology used in this area can be confusing.

Illustration 1.1　Starting a small consultancy business

> For 20 years Peter ran a small (one person) consultancy business. Earlier in his life the thought of having his own business had never occurred to him, but at one time he worked for a small business support agency – a job which entailed encouraging other people to start businesses. Therefore, when a restructuring of the agency led to him being made redundant, he felt obliged to try it himself – although he did also keep an eye on the local job market in case any attractive jobs were advertised.
>
> During his time in the agency two people with whom he had been working had started their own consultancy businesses and this

was something he thought he could try also. Therefore he set up as a 'sole trader' using a computer and desk at home. He also ordered business cards and headed paper, registered for self-employment National Insurance, and advertised his services in general terms in Yellow Pages.

Shortly after starting up he was approached, separately, by two clients of the agency he had worked for who asked if he could help them to prepare their applications for agency support. He checked with his former colleagues and they encouraged him to go ahead, pointing out that they wanted to assist these clients, but needed plans with their submissions. He should be able to write plans which met all the agency's requirements.

Thinking about this, he realised that, having worked on awarding grants, he was well placed to help people to apply for grants because he knew how the grant-givers thought and what information they needed. Thus he developed this as one of his areas of expertise. He found customers mainly through networking and word of mouth. Through the same media he also found indications of other services that he might offer. His business prospered to the extent that he stopped looking for other possible employment elsewhere. As the service he offered depended largely on his own contacts, experience and knowledge, he remained a one-person business, but he did sometimes collaborate with other self-employed people to work on larger projects. After a while his turnover grew to the level at which he needed to register for VAT, and after a couple of years (at his accountant's suggestion) he formed a limited company which took over the business's activities and acquired its goodwill. Officially he became its only employee.

Relatively early in this process he was asked, in a survey of new small businesses, what his business aims were. This made him think about them and he recorded them as follows, and in no particular order:

- To generate enough income to maintain his standard of living.

- To make a contribution to the local community.

- To enjoy his business activity.

He did not see the need subsequently to change these aims. He had seen a possibility for a business, made a start, used his contacts and built on opportunities when he found them, established a diverse client base, and clarified his objectives – and, as a result, the business sustained him until he reached retirement age while meeting his objectives for it. It was thus a successful venture.

*Source*: Based on S. Bridge and K. O'Neill, *Understanding Enterprise Entrepreneurship and Small Business* (Basingstoke: Palgrave Macmillan, 4th edn 2013) p. 249.

This is a book for people who want to create a new venture: people who, instead of being content always to wait for other people to do things, want to see what they can do themselves to create something helpful. That might be something that helps them personally – for instance by creating their own business because working for someone else does not provide enough income and/or job satisfaction (see, for example, Illustration 1.1); it might be something that helps a group to which they belong or the community in which they live (see, for example, Illustration 1.4); or it might be something they want to do to help other people – for instance by launching a new charity to provide aid for the victims of a disaster. All these are valid new ventures.

Illustration 1.2   Examples of enterprising ventures

As well as many examples of people starting small businesses or establishing freelance careers (see, for example Illustration 1.1), the following are also examples of enterprising ventures:

- Starting a series of car boot sales
- Devising a new academic course
- Establishing a community centre
- Opening a local tea shop
- Campaigning to save a local school
- Launching a new family support group
- Putting on a theatrical production
- Developing a new medical procedure

# The Purpose of this Book

> - Forming a youth club
> - Forming a local art group
> - Forming a building preservation trust (Illustration 1.4)
> - Campaigning for a change in the law

'An enterprise' it has been said, 'is a goal-realisation device'.[1] The enterprises listed in Illustration 1.2 are ventures which are designed to help people to achieve their goals. Some of those enterprises or ventures might be described as businesses (see Illustration 1.3), but whatever they are called they should be seen as the means to an end – not as ends in themselves. If the enterprises concerned are not going to help to achieve those goals, why pursue them?

Illustration 1.3  Enterprise terminology

> There are many words which can be used to describe a new initiative of the sort described in this chapter, and many of those words can be used in a variety of ways because they don't have single, clear, narrow definitions. Some of the words may apply only to some initiatives and not to others, and some can have adverse connotations because they are perceived by some to apply to initiatives of which they do not approve.
>
> For instance, a few years ago it might have been assumed that any new economic venture

would have been a new business, and if this book had been written then it would probably have described itself as a business start-up guide. However, many new ventures are not businesses and are not likely to become businesses later. Although businesses are often described as enterprises, not all enterprising ventures can be described as businesses. Businesses are often thought to be private trading enterprises launched for personal financial gain – but then there are social enterprises and community businesses to which that does not apply. Businesses are also thought to be founded by entrepreneurs – a term sometimes thought to refer to people whose sole interest is in making as much money as possible for themselves, even if it is at the expense of others. (See also the Further Information section for more on terminology).

Thus selecting an appropriate vocabulary for this book is not easy. Saying that it is about entrepreneurs and their new businesses would be too limiting, and the terms 'business' and 'entrepreneur' can have negative connotations for some people. 'Enterprise' is a possibility, but 'enterprising people' would be too broad. So instead this book talks about 'ventures', and refers to those people who are exploring the possibility of a new venture as 'new venture explorers'.

Do you have a goal which might be achieved by a new venture? If so, this book is for you. It is a book for new venture explorers (in the terminology suggested in Illustration 1.3) – that is, people who want to find a way to develop a new venture, which might be self-employment and/or a business, but might also be something else, such as a new club, or society or charity. However, whatever it is, its essence is that the people concerned are prepared to take the initiative in doing it, because it would not otherwise happen.

Being able to launch a new venture – to start a new initiative rather than just hitching a ride on an existing one – is potentially a very useful ability. A new venture is inevitably something of a step into the unknown because the future is uncertain and not pre-ordained. A new venture is thus a form of exploration, and while exploration cannot be planned in detail in advance, it can be guided – and this book suggests a set of principles to guide such ventures. And new ventures will not happen unless new venture explorers are prepared to take the initiative to explore and make them happen.

First, however, this part of the book explores what guidance is already available and compares that with the real needs of small new ventures. It starts by looking at the business plan, which is often advocated. However, as explained above, a new venture does not necessarily have to be an embryonic business and, even if a new business is contemplated, a business plan is not necessarily the best tool to use. Similarly, other available guidance, although it may contain some useful points, is also generally limited in its application.

Therefore, to provide guidance applicable to most, if not all, new ventures, this book suggests a set of 10 guiding principles. Part I considers the needs of new venturers and the guidance available from other sources in order to identify a set of guiding principles of new venturing. Those principles are then described in more detail in Part II.

**Illustration 1.4    Holywood Old School**

> The Old School on Church Road in the small town of Holywood in County Down was built in 1845 as the Parochial National School. It continued in use as a school until 1878, when a new and bigger Parochial School on the opposite side of the road was opened. It was then used as a parish hall and, from 1916, was also used as a scout hall. However, by the beginning of this century even this use had ceased for safety reasons due to deterioration of the fabric of the hall, and the building was under threat of demolition to provide a development site.
> 
> But many people in Holywood did not want to lose the Old School building because it had become part of the town's history. It was one of the first buildings to be constructed above the early town, it contributed to the visual appearance of Church Road and it had made a big contribution to education and young people in Holywood.
> 
> Therefore, following discussions about the future of the building with the Church of Ireland, which owns the building, a group of local people agreed to form a Building Preservation Trust to try to secure its future. In this they had two objectives:
> 
> - A conservation objective, which was to retain as much as possible of the original fabric of

the building and to conserve both its outward and inward appearance.

- A viability objective, which was to find a sustainable use, or mix of uses, for the building which would be both consistent with the conservation requirement and of direct benefit to the community in Holywood.

As a result, in April 2004 the Holywood Old School Preservation Trust was incorporated as a company limited by guarantee and registered as a charity. Its first initiative was to raise money for, and then to commission, a feasibility study. This produced a positive result indicating that the building could be restored and might then have a sustainable future – so the Trust decided to proceed and a full fundraising campaign was launched to pay for the relevant conservation work. The Trust was then able to re-open the building in 2008 and, since then, the Old School has operated sustainably, providing premises for a variety of community groups and activities and earning enough from that to pay for all its running costs.

### Summary of the Key Points of Chapter 1

- An enterprise, it has been said, is a goal realisation device, and this is a book for new venture explorers – people who want to explore a new venture as a way to achieve their goals.

- New ventures can take many forms, including, but not limited to, new businesses.

- However, the terminology used, including concepts such as ventures and enterprises, businesses and entrepreneurs, can be confusing.

- New ventures will not happen unless new venture explorers are prepared to take the initiative to make them happen.

# 2
# Business Plans – Why Are They Advocated?

> **The Essence of This Chapter**
> - Business plans are often advised as an essential requirement for new ventures.
> - The likely origins of the 'business plan' lie in the tendency among business 'professionals' to apply big business thinking.
> - There are reasons why professionals like business plans and often advocate them.

## BUSINESS PLANS ARE OFTEN ADVOCATED

Illustration 2.1   Some advice for people starting businesses

| | |
|---|---|
| From banks: | 'If you intend to start a business you need to write a business plan.'[1]<br>'Writing a business plan is one of the most important tasks when starting up a new business.'[2] |

| | |
|---|---|
| From entrepreneurship text books: | 'One of the most important steps in setting up any new business is to develop a business plan.'[3] <br> 'It has become accepted that a carefully constructed business plan is important to the survival and successful performance of any business.'[4] |
| From start-up guides: | 'Every business needs a business plan ... To do this you'll have to take a long hard look at each element of the plan.'[5] <br> 'It is essential to have a realistic, working business plan when you're starting up a business.'[6] |
| From business development agencies: | 'To start a business – you'll need a business plan.'[7] <br> 'A business plan is one of the most important documents any start-up business can invest in and writing one is one of the most important things a business owner can go through.'[8] |

If you seek advice about starting a new venture it is very likely that you will be told that you need a business plan, especially if you describe your new venture as a business. There is very widespread agreement that a business plan is essential for a new venture (see Illustration 2.1) and therefore the first guidance this book considers is the business plan. However, Chapter 3 suggests that this view is wrong and that business plans are often not helpful for new ventures. But before that, this chapter examines why business plans are advocated so often. If the standard advice is wrong and if business plans as normally formulated are often not only unhelpful but even harmful for new ventures, why are they so frequently recommended? Instead of just stating that they are wrong, this section explains why they seem to be so popular – because understanding the reasons for their popularity may help people to resist them when they are suggested.

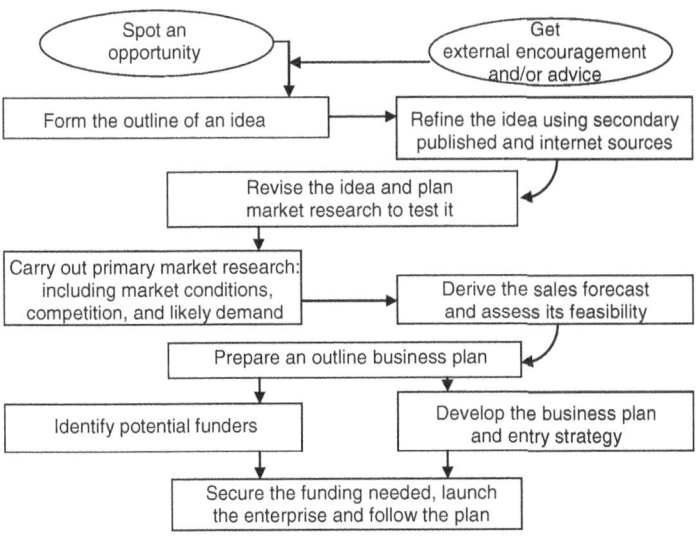

Figure 2.1 *Business start-up: The strategic planning process*

*Source*: Based on S. Bridge and K. O'Neill, *Understanding Enterprise, Entrepreneurship and Small Business* (Basingstoke: Palgrave, 4th edn 2013) p. 240.

## WHAT IS A BUSINESS PLAN?

Many sources will provide guides for preparing a business plan – with a lot in common among their various suggestions. In explaining what a business plan is, however, it might be useful to look at the process which is supposed to be undertaken in launching a new business venture. This is shown in diagrammatic form in Figure 2.1 and summarised in Table 2.1.

In essence a business plan records the key points in this process and a typical layout for it is given in Table 2.2.

Table 2.1 *The start-up strategic process*

Ten steps can be identified in the strategic planning process for a new venture, of which the business plan forms a key component:

1. Identify a business idea (because it seems promising, trendy, appropriate for you etc.).
2. Investigate its market – will it sell, in what volumes, under what conditions, and for what price? Also, what is the competition and on what factors do they compete?
3. Determine what you will need in the way of premises, equipment, stock, organisation, staff, marketing campaign etc. – and their cost.
4. Plan the sequencing of actions and spends.
5. Prepare financial projections – what level of profit should the venture make, and what investment is required?
6. Write up all that in a business plan (in a form that is ready to present to potential supporters and/or investors).
7. Review your analysis and its conclusions and decide whether or not to go ahead.
8. Raise the investment needed.
9. Start.
10. Follow the plan.

Table 2.2 *A business plan layout*

The following is a typical layout for a business plan:

**The executive summary:** A summary of the key points in the plan.

**Introduction to the business:** What is it about? Who is involved? What were the origins of the idea? What is the basic proposal? How was it developed? What form will the business take? What is the present position? What is the aim?

**The product(s) or service(s):** What does the business propose to offer? What is the product or service and what are its key features? What has been done to test that it works? How will it be produced or supplied?

**The market:** How will the offering be received? What is the size and growth rate of the market? Where is the market? What is the customer profile? What is the competition? What do customers really want from the product/service? What will be the competitive edge? What is the evidence that there will be a demand for the offering? What price levels prevail?

**Costing and pricing and the sales forecast:** How much will the business be able to sell (*the sales forecast*)? What will be the cost of producing at this level (for material, labour and overheads)? What price will be put on the product or service?

**Operations plan:** How will the product or service be produced? What equipment will be needed? What premises/space will be needed? What will be the best location?

**Marketing and sales plan:** How will customers be persuaded to buy your product or service? What distribution channel(s) will be used? What selling and what promotional activity will be needed? What will the promotion and distribution look like?

**Organisation and staffing:** What business structure will be established? Where will the business be based? What staff will be needed? What skills are critical to success and what rates of remuneration will be paid? How will the business be managed?

**Financial forecasts:** The financial aspects of all this are then put together to produce financial projections for the business.

**Other points:** Although not always included in business plan formats, a risk assessment and a summary of the projected benefits can also help to persuade people to support the plan.

## THE ORIGINS OF THE BUSINESS PLAN

Where does this enthusiasm for business plans come from? It has been suggested that business plans were invented by bank managers[9] because they so often ask for them or, if not by them, then by accountants or consultants who often seem to know how to do them. It has also been suggested that business schools like them because they bring together all the main strands of business school teaching – such as marketing, operations management, organisational behaviour, and finance and accounting. Bank managers, accountants and business consultants could be described as business professionals, not because they have businesses of their own, but because knowing about businesses is part of their professional understanding, which they apply on a professional basis to businesses owned by others. A list of such professionals might also include business academics, business trainers, the staff of business development agencies and the hired managers of bigger businesses – and all of them seem to like business plans – for instance:

- Banks like them because a business plan can provide the basis for assessing loan requests.

- Business trainers like them because the business plan's contents offer a seemingly logical framework and approved syllabus for start-up training.

- Business support agencies like them because a business plan should provide all the key information about the business and its prospects needed to justify any offer of help.

- Business schools like them because, as suggested above, a business plan can provide an exercise which brings together inputs from (almost) all the main areas of business school teaching.

What many of these professionals have in common, as well as a love of business plans, is that they have generally learnt about businesses from a big business model – because that is the basis for the received wisdom about business. Instead of having personal experience of working in a small business, they have acquired their business understanding by working in a big business, learning from colleagues who have acquired a big business perspective and/or being taught by people who have in turn studied or been taught big business approaches. Thus they have learnt that businesses are comprised of separate functions, such as R&D, marketing and sales, operations and money management – because in big businesses these are often carried out in separate departments. They have also learnt that businesses not only should, but generally do, make logical, objective decisions about how to maximise their profitability.

Illustration 2.2   Two parallel views on small businesses

> An example of the development of conventional business wisdom is the first business textbook recommended to one of the authors. It was *Business Enterprise: Its Growth and Organisation*, by Ronald Edwards and Harry Townsend[10] and it was first published in 1958. One of its interesting features now is more what it doesn't say about

business than what it does say. For instance, it does indicate that some businesses are small and that smallness can have advantages because flexibility and ease of control can be lost when firms get larger and gain economies of scale. But it does not have a section on small businesses, and it gives no indication that they are otherwise different or worthy of special attention.

However, that book was followed in the very next year by *The Theory of the Growth of the Firm*, by Edith Penrose, which does point out that small businesses are very different from big businesses. Penrose specifically examined what happened as firms grew and, according to her:

> What has happened as firms have grown larger is not that they have become inefficient, but that with increasing size both the managerial function and the basic administrative structure have undergone fundamental changes which profoundly affect the nature of the 'organism' itself. The differences in the administrative structure of the very small and the very large firms are so great that in many ways it is hard to see that the two species are of the same genus. We say they are because they both fulfil the same function, yet they certainly fulfil it differently, and it may be that in time the differences will become so great that we should consider in what sense they can both be called industrial 'firms'. In other words,

> I think the question whether firms can get 'too big' for efficiency is the wrong question, for there is no reason to assume that as the large firms grow larger and larger they will become inefficient; it is much more likely that their organization will become so different that we must look on them differently; we cannot define a caterpillar and then use the same definition for a butterfly.[11]
>
> Thus Penrose did point out that there were fundamental differences between small and large businesses. But, while many people acknowledge this, they do not seem to have reset their default thinking. Although they may 'know' that small businesses are different they have not changed the business thinking which they have acquired and which continues to follow the approach exemplified by Edwards and Townsend rather than the radical ideas of people like Penrose.

Although it was over 50 years ago that Penrose observed that as firms grow larger they become 'so different that we must look on them differently',[12] many people still do not seem to have grasped the importance of that observation. It is as if, once the word 'business' is mentioned, they switch on their standard business thinking and assume that it is relevant – having failed to realise that much of it is inappropriate for small businesses. They seem to have forgotten, if they had ever learnt, that small businesses are not small big businesses, even though they are both referred to as 'businesses', and that many new ventures may not even become established businesses. Thus many business 'professionals' unthinkingly and/or unconsciously apply a perspective based on big businesses.

That big-business-based perspective includes the usefulness of the business plan. Bigger businesses should not launch large-scale new ventures without some form of prior research and planning. Because the investment required is likely to be large and the contributions of many people will need to be coordinated, some prior feasibility assessment and resource marshalling is likely to be necessary. Nevertheless, even when this is done, things can still go wrong, as happened when Coca-Cola tried to reformulate and relaunch its basic product because market research had suggested that customers preferred the taste of the revised version. If you are going to try to lead a large number of people through a piece of unfamiliar territory, it helps to reconnoitre it first to ascertain what is likely to be the best route and then to record that route so that others can understand it – and that is what the business planning process can do.

## WHY PROFESSIONALS LIKE BUSINESS PLANS

Professionals may have learnt that business plans are what businesses should do. They are the approved method, they clearly conform to the establishment view, they are what other people advocate and, in any case, most people appear to see no alternative. It is therefore not surprising that they are often advocated – and they have other advantages too, including:

- They support an approach based on analysing the component parts or activities of a business.

This is the way that professionals are often taught to view businesses, and business plans provide a very good exercise in that approach. For instance, as indicated above, business schools teach subjects like marketing, operations management and finance, and therefore a business plan, which has sections on each of those components, is going to be seen as a good exercise for practising them.

- Business plans provide an apparently logical[13] basis for analysis and/or support decisions (and they do so in a form that is easily recorded and kept on file). For accountants and consultants they provide a generally approved and accepted framework for analysis, and for bankers and business agency staff they provide a very useful way of presenting and recording an analysis of the business and the reason why it should be supported – or not, as the case may be.

- Business plans provide an accepted, and apparently logical,[14] structure for teaching the start-up process – and an easy basis for grading the acquisition of that learning. It is relatively easy to set and score assignments based on the business plan and also to accredit the learning syllabus. Even if trainers do not actually advocate doing business plans, the subjects they teach are often based on the standard components of a plan, which therefore form the basis and syllabus for many start-up guidance schemes and training courses, again because that fits the established view of what is relevant. And another result of the business plan's hegemony is that often those schemes and courses only cover what is in the business plan.

- Business plans help the cautious, and what the professionals all have in common is an inclination towards caution. They probably feel that they have more to lose from an association with failure than they might stand to gain if a business they advise or support is a roaring success. Association with a failure would mean the loss of a loan or of credibility, whereas major success would bring no extra compensating concrete benefit. Thus they would probably rather a business did not start at all if there were a significant possibility of failure.

- Business plans provide a valued source of income for those professionals who are hired to teach them – or to prepare them for prospective start-ups who have been told they need one but do not have the time, the understanding or the patience to do it for themselves.

Therefore, probably because they have been taught that they are the right thing to do, because business plans suit their purposes well, because everyone else seems to advocate them, and because they often see no alternative, business plans have become the tool of choice for many business professionals who are supposed to be helping start-ups – even if they are not actually helpful to those start-ups themselves. As a result, this has given added currency to the notion that the business plan is the essential first step for all start-ups and that its contents should form the basis of the syllabus for start-up guidance schemes and training courses.

## Summary of the Key Points of Chapter 2

- Business plans are frequently advocated as essential for new business ventures.

- Business plans seem to have been invented by business professionals who deal with small businesses and start-ups mainly on a professional basis rather than as active owners of the ventures.

- Those business professionals have probably learnt about business from a big business perspective. Although they may have heard that small businesses are not small big businesses, their default thinking is nevertheless big-business-based.

- Business plans conform to establishment thinking and are in many other ways helpful to business professionals.

# 3
# Are Business Plans Appropriate?

> **The Essence of This Chapter**
> - There is evidence that business plans do not help new ventures.
> - At the heart of business plans are sales forecasts – which are highly suspect.
> - There is now considerable scepticism about business plans and even start-up training based on business plan contents has been called into question.

## CHALLENGING THE RELEVANCE OF THE BUSINESS PLAN

The previous section described how the business plan has become the standard advice given by business professionals to anyone starting a new venture. The business plan approach, it seems, has achieved this dominance in professional thinking because it helps business professionals with their agenda and accords with their understanding of business, and because such professionals appear to see no alternatives. But the relevance and usefulness of business plans for new small businesses are now being challenged.

Illustration 3.1   Do business plans help new ventures?

> Many people who are starting new ventures do not feel that business plans are a help, and they either do them reluctantly or don't do them at all. Babson College in Massachusetts, USA, is widely known for its entrepreneurship teaching. However, a survey conducted in 2009 of former students of Babson who had graduated between 1985 and 2006, and who had since then founded one or more full-time new ventures, found that in only about half of the cases had those former students prepared a written business plan before the business began operating. The survey also concluded that overall the subsequent performance of all the new ventures was *not* related to having such a business plan.[1]
>
> Another survey was conducted by Tjan *et al.*, the authors of *Heart, Smarts Guts and Luck*, who report that in the course of their research they asked entrepreneurs across the globe how they launched their businesses. 'Of those that had successful exits', they found, 'nearly 70 per cent did *not* start with a business plan.'[2]
>
> But the behaviour of the Babson alumni and these other entrepreneurs was not discovered until later, when specific research was done into the value of business planning. Indeed there are many other examples found by the authors in the course of writing this book which indicate that people who have not prepared business plans tend not to declare it publicly.

> Possibly they have kept quiet about this because they feel that they should have prepared plans when they are advocated by apparent experts. Or sometimes they want a loan or other support from the professional advocating the plans and they don't want to offend them by disagreeing. Therefore they may just get on with doing things their way, thinking that they are a rare exception to the rule that a business plan is necessary. Thus they may think that, at least from their perspective, the emperor has no clothes – but they don't want to appear foolish or give offence by saying so.

Business plans appear to be based on big business thinking but, as Edith Penrose pointed out over 50 years ago, small businesses are not small big businesses and do not behave like them. Nevertheless many of us seem to have been hooked by the word 'business' – automatically switching on and/or applying big-business-based thinking to anything that is labelled a business – and along with that big-business-based thinking go business plans.

But the value and the apparent hegemony of business plans are now being questioned – and for at least four reasons:

- Firstly there is a lack of reliable evidence that business plans actually help businesses. Where research has been conducted into the efficacy of planning for businesses this has not been conclusive. Henry Mintzberg reviewed the evidence for his book on strategic planning and found that, 'at the very least ... planning is not the "one best way" and that it certainly does not pay in general'[3]. Illustration 3.1 also includes summaries of two pieces of more recent research on the specific application of business plans to successful start-ups which also failed to find a conclusive link.

- Secondly a number of academics who have worked with small businesses and business plans have queried the relevance of the latter. Some of this is summarised in Illustration 3.2 and comes mainly from their own observations rather than from after–the-event research looking for correlations.

- Thirdly there are questions about the validity of the business plan process. At the heart of a business plan is a sales forecast upon which the estimates of future costs, revenues and profitability are based. But those sales forecasts are usually based on market research – which is not reliable (as Illustration 3.3 indicates). The only credible way to see if people will buy something is to offer it to them and see what happens. Without that sort of real-life testing the edifice of a business plan is built on sand.

- Fourthly, as explained above, business plans are based on big business thinking, but, as Penrose pointed out, small businesses are very different from big businesses and do not behave like small versions of big businesses. Therefore it is not necessarily the case that what suits big businesses will suit smaller ones.

Illustration 3.2  Business plan scepticism

| | |
|---|---|
| An academic paper: | 'An intense debate emerged recently ... on the value of business planning for established small and especially new firms.'[4] |
| An entrepreneurship educator: | 'We have all heard the growing chorus ... debating the proper role, if any, for teaching business plans. A valid criticism ... is that the way business plans have been traditionally taught results in well-written "works of fiction".'[5] |
| An entrepreneurship professor and author: | 'I am more than ever convinced that entrepreneurship cannot be planned to any major extent in advance, and that planning even goes against the entrepreneurial idea. Entrepreneurship is rather about courage and willpower, being venturesome when experimenting and networking, and about exploiting necessary mistakes as moments of learning.'[6] |
| An entrepreneurship professor emeritus: | 'My focus ... is on a number of "elephants in the room" ... such as the worship of the rational business plan in curricula.'[7] |

| An associate professor and participant in eight high-tech start-ups | 'We've now learned [that]…: <br><br>• Business plans rarely survive first contact with customers. … <br><br>• No one besides venture capitalists and the late Soviet Union requires five year plans to forecast complete unknowns.'[8] |
|---|---|

Illustration 3.3   The limitations of market forecasting

> Often we think we can forecast the future, not least because, as Daniel Kahneman has pointed out, our ability to construct coherent narratives of the past leads us to think we could do the same for the future:
>
>> Everything makes sense in hindsight, a fact that financial pundits exploit every evening as they offer convincing accounts of the day's events. And we cannot suppress the powerful intuition that what makes sense in hindsight today was predictable yesterday. The illusion that we understand the past fosters overconfidence in our ability to predict the future.[9]

But even in a limited area like market research our ability to forecast the future is indeed more an illusion than a reality. In his book *Consumer.ology*, Philip Graves shows that 'market research cannot work'. According to the book's cover:

> Philip Graves, one of the world's leading experts in consumer behavior, reveals why the findings obtained from most market research are completely unreliable. Whether it is company executives seeking to define their corporate strategy or politicians wanting to understand the electorate, the idea that questions answered on a questionnaire or discussed in a focus group can provide useful insights on which to base business decisions is the cause of product failures, political blunders and wasted billions.[10]

However, the basis of the business plan approach is a sales forecast often based on just such market research. Upon that sales forecast the production requirements, the staffing needed and the marketing plan are all established and on them the financial requirements are projected and the businesses viability assessed. Yet, according to Philip Graves:

> The fundamental tenet of market research is that you can ask people questions and that what they tell you in response will be true. [But] ... this is a largely baseless

> belief [and] in fact it turns out that the opposite is far closer to the truth.[11]

This is because:

> The nature of a conscious response says much about a respondent's conscious values and how they would like to perceive themselves, but can reveal very little about what really has driven their behavior in the past or what they will do in the future. For example, there are thousands of people each year who resolve not to overeat; they generate a well-intentioned conscious response to the tightness of a favorite pair of jeans, or their doctor's health warning. However, only a small proportion of these people will develop sustained new eating and exercising behaviors. This is not because their conscious intention was insincere, but because the unconscious drive to eat in response to particular physical or emotional stimulus will cut in and trigger consumption irrespective of their conscious intent.[12]

Thus the apparent benefits of the business plan for start-ups are being queried. After reviewing the evidence it seems reasonable to conclude that, while business plans may help business professionals, they do not necessarily help actual new venture explorers.

## WHAT PLANNING AND GUIDANCE ARE RELEVANT?

### The Role of Planning

Although the relevance of business plans for small businesses is being queried, even small businesses, and other enterprising ventures, still need to do some planning. As has been said: 'almost all work, in order to be done at all, must be planned, at least informally and a few minutes ahead.'[13] You can't even make a cup of tea without determining, even if only from custom and practice, in which order to do things. If the kettle is not boiled before the water is added to the tea the brew doesn't work. If you are boiling an egg, you need to allow enough time for the egg to boil if it is to be cooked. If you are sending a letter it needs to be written before it is posted. Thus even simple tasks like these need to be planned – even if only informally and only a little while in advance. Larger tasks, such as building a new sports stadium or carrying out a military invasion, such as that of D-Day, require much more planning.

But there is a difference between planning activities like making a cup of tea or even building a new sports stadium and planning to invade France on D-Day – and that is the predictability of the conditions in which it will be done. Generally making a cup of tea is a very predictable event (although unexpected power cuts can happen), but D-Day was different – it depended on both the weather and German reaction, and both of those were very uncertain.

In planning circles there are generally two main approaches to planning for uncertain conditions. One approach, exemplified by many business plans, is to rely on prior analysis and market research to remove, or at lease reduce, any uncertainty. However, the future is inherently unpredictable (and Illustration 3.3 describes one area in which attempts to try to predict it are known to be unreliable). Sometimes, for a while, the future behaves as might be expected, where present trends are continued, but often, at some time or another, it is subject to turbulence and to sudden unforeseeable shocks. Thus the second approach to operating in uncertain conditions is to try to be ready to respond when the unexpected occurs.

Planning can seek to provide or assist with several functions including thinking about the future, trying to control the future, making decisions and coordinating actions. But this chapter suggests that, at least for new small ventures, trying to reduce future uncertainty by analysis and research is unlikely to work and therefore plans based on such assumptions are unlikely to be realistic. However, small ventures need to do some checking and planning, even if only to ensure that what they are trying to do has some chance of working and is not fatally flawed by issues which could be checked. It does not take much planning, for instance, to verify that the price that might be charged for an item or service will be enough to cover the likely costs of producing it – but going beyond that to assume how many will be sold could be stretching the validity of planning beyond its limits.

Military plans, for instance, generally do not last unchanged beyond the first contact with the enemy – then the forces concerned need to respond to the situation as it evolves, which requires different thinking. As General Sir Frederick Morgan, who was responsible for much of the D-Day planning, is reputed to have observed: 'whereas anyone can make a plan, it takes something quite out of the ordinary to carry it out'. So the people concerned need to plan their preparation but then also be able to respond to the unforeseen. You can't plan in advance the detail of how you will respond to the unforeseen – because it is unforeseen – and an over-reliance on planning can lead some into a sort of blinkered attitude which does not appear to recognise the relevance of anything unforeseen because it has not been forecast in the plan.

**Appropriate Guidance**

As its name suggests, the business plan approach provides businesses with a planning process. However, the standard business plan format is also used as an indication of the key considerations for a new start-up – and thus the issues on which some guidance might be helpful. Thus advice, guidance and training for new business start-ups are often based on the components of a business plan, and if something doesn't normally feature in a business plan it doesn't get advised or taught. (Compare Illustration 3.4 with Table 2.2 – while the lists in each case are not identical there is little in the guidance list in Illustration 3.4 that does not relate to one or more of the items in the business plan list in Table 2.2, p. 17.)

Illustration 3.4  The business plan as a start-up syllabus

> The following are the chapter headings in a business start-up guide. It is suggested that they bear

a close resemblance to the components of a business plan and therefore that they were probably derived from business plan thinking:

Introduction

1. Starting a business

2. Forming a business

3. Marketing and sales

4. Managing your money

5. Where to work

6. The legal bit

7. Selling yourself

8. Mentors and role models

9. Going for growth

10. Writing a business plan

Conclusion

*Source*: Prince's Trust, *Make It Happen: The Prince's Trust Guide to Starting Your Own Business* (Chichester: Capstone Publishing Ltd, 2011).

But new ventures need some planning and guidance. Business plans, and any guidance based on them, may be relevant for big businesses, but, as pointed out above, small businesses are not small big businesses – and many new ventures are not (yet) even businesses. So what is appropriate for them?

## REVIEW

Business plans are advocated not because they are actually best for new ventures, but because they are good for the advocates and suit their thinking. The previous section indicates that business professionals usually derive their understanding of businesses from studies of how big businesses operate. Big businesses use business plans and business plans are frequently helpful to those professionals. Therefore business plans are frequently advocated by business 'professionals' as necessary for any new business venture. They are advised as the only approach available and thus they also form the basis for much business start-up preparation advice and for training courses.

Business plans clearly conform to the established view and are part of the conventional wisdom. They are widely accepted by the established authorities as being helpful for businesses. Thus anyone who advocates them is unlikely to be criticised by that establishment. As John Kenneth Galbraith, who is credited with inventing the term 'conventional wisdom', said:

> We associate truth with convenience – with what most closely accords with self-interest and personal well-being or promises best to avoid awkward effort or unwelcome dislocation

of life. ... But perhaps most important of all, people approve most of what they best understand. As just noted, economic and social behavior are complex, and to comprehend their character is mentally tiring. Therefore we adhere, as though to a raft, to those ideas which represent our understanding. ... It is why men react, not infrequently with something akin to religious passion, to the defense of what they have so laboriously learned.'[14]

But as Penrose indicated (see Illustration 2.2) small businesses are not like small big businesses – they behave and operate very differently – and big business guidance is not necessarily appropriate for them. Therefore, instead of just assuming that big business methods such as business plans are appropriate, it is relevant to look at what guidance those involved in new ventures might actually need.

---

Summary of the Key Points of Chapter 3

- There is evidence that business plans do not help new ventures, even when those ventures take the form of businesses.
- Business plans depend on sale forecasts – but such market research is often not reliable.
- For these and other reasons the value of business plans is now being questioned.
- Business plans provide not only a planning mechanism but also a syllabus for start-up training – so that syllabus is also suspect.

# 4
# Business Plans Are Not the Only Option

> **The Essence of This Chapter**
> - Although business plans have become the standard advice for start-ups, they are not necessarily appropriate.
> - There are other guides for early stage ventures, although often with limited application.
> - Many successful entrepreneurs follow an effectual approach and this is consistent with seeing start-up as a form of exploration.

## ALTERNATIVE GUIDES

If business plans are often not an appropriate guide for a new venture, then what is? The answer is that there is not one single approach which is best in all circumstances and there are a number of guides each with their own particular advantages relevant to different circumstances. Thus, instead of having just one tool to use in all circumstances, there is a selection of different tools, each with different uses.

For among the other guides or methods which have been offered, three are reviewed here:

- *A Better Mousetrap* (see Illustration 4.1)
- *So what? who cares? why you?* (see Illustration 4.2)
- Lean Startup (see Illustration 4.3)

Illustration 4.1   *A Better Mousetrap*

> *A Better Mousetrap*,[1] sub-titled '*a guide for inventors*', is a guide for people who think they have invented something and want to see how it might be turned into a commercial product.
> 
> It has sections on:
> 
> - Is the idea original?
> - Is there a demand for it?
> - Will it work?
> - Will there be anything worth selling?
> - Intellectual property
> - Financial expectation, and
> - Commercial strategy.
> 
> It is thus relevant to inventors to help them to see if their invention is worth developing further but it does not cover the business start-up process.

Illustration 4.2   *So what? who cares? why you?*

> *So what? who cares? why you?* by Wendy Kennedy[2] is described as 'the inventor's

commercialisation toolkit' and is aimed at 'scientists, researchers, engineers and technology entrepreneurs' to help to 'turn your good idea into a great opportunity'. On the presumption that innovations often come with mountains of technical detail but fail to show what the business opportunity in the idea is, this method is designed to clarify and highlight the 'business value proposition'.

It covers:

- So what? – What is the idea, what problem does it solve and where does it fit?

- Who cares? – Who is the customer, what's the path to market and where's the money?

- Why you? – What is your competitive edge, who's on your team and what's your story?

This method thus starts with the assumption that the idea is worth developing and covers the key issues to be addressed in commercialising it, assuming some form of business start-up.

Illustration 4.3   Lean Startup

Lean Startup is an approach to business formation and development formulated by Eric Ries as a development of Steve Blank's Customer Development methodology. He found that, instead of going to all the cost of trying to

> produce a final fully developed product before launching it on real customers, it was generally better to try an early version of the product on a few customers to get their reaction. That could be very helpful in identifying which features most appealed to customers and which were not appreciated or needed further development.
>
> Lean Startup relies on a scientific approach to experimentation combined with a series of iterative product releases to gain valuable customer feedback and shorten product development cycles. In this way start-ups can design products or services to meet the demands of customers without requiring lots of initial funding or expensive product launches.
>
> Lean Startup was originally developed in Silicon Valley for high-technology software companies but – not least through the success of Ries's book[3] – the philosophy has since been applied to businesses in other sectors that seek to develop innovative new products for the marketplace. (See also Illustration 12.2, p. 113.)

So, instead of the business plan being the only way, other guides are available, although none of them seems to have universal application. *A Better Mousetrap* is primarily aimed at inventors, *So what? Who cares? Why you?* is designed for innovations and Lean Startup was developed for high-tech businesses in Silicon Valley, although it is now being applied more widely.

There is another approach which is worthy of consideration, and that is effectuation (see Illustration 4.4).

However, rather than being developed initially as a guide, effectuation has its origins in observations of how successful real entrepreneurs actually work. The studies on which it was based found that successful entrepreneurs frequently did not follow causal approaches consistent with business plans and indeed distrusted the sort of market research on which business plans are based. Effectuation has also subsequently been used as the basis for what is described as a 'vivid new way to learn about and to practice entrepreneurship'[4].

Illustration 4.4   Effectuation

> Saras Sarasvathy studied how entrepreneurs actually operate – as opposed to how they were thought to operate. She interviewed 27 'expert' entrepreneurs: people 'who, either individually or as part of a team, had founded one or more companies, had remained a full-time founder/entrepreneur for ten years or more and participated in taking at least one company public'.[5] She found that most of the time, when contemplating a new venture, they did not do a lot of market research and extensive pre-planning. They distrusted market research and revealed 'a profound distrust of attempts to predict the future'[6] and they did not try to plan the shape of the venture in advance and then try to implement those plans.
>
> Instead they mainly followed a process, not of 'causation', but of 'effectuation'. Traditionally, she suggests, entrepreneurs were thought to pursue a causal approach in which they fix on a target and then try to cause it to happen, whereas effectuation

starts with the means available and then proceeds to see what can be made from that. Causation is like doing a jigsaw puzzle – where you start with a picture of the final result you are aiming to create and then look for and put into position just those pieces that will construct it. Effectuation, on the other hand, is like making a patchwork quilt where you start by looking at what pieces are available and where the nature of the pieces you find helps to determine what the final result will look like. Also, as Sarasvathy points out, a finished patchwork quilt is often much more useful than a completed jigsaw puzzle.

If making a jigsaw puzzle is causation, so is making a model aircraft from a kit of preformed pieces which can only make the specific aircraft in question. The model or toy-maker's horizons are thus limited to the predetermined outcome. However, with a Lego toy aircraft it is possible either to follow the instructions and construct the toy as shown on the box or to use the same pieces in an effectual way to construct a different toy if that is what is desired.

Sarasvathy suggested that the five key principles of effectuation are:

> The *bird-in-hand* principle – Effectuation is means-driven, rather than goal-driven. Its emphasis is on creating something new with existing means rather than on devising new means to chosen goals.
>
> The *affordable loss* principle – Instead of making a business-plan-based on sales

projections and trying to raise the investment the expected returns appear to justify, this principle indicates that your commitment to a venture should be limited to no more than you can afford to lose on it.

The *crazy-quilt* principle – Effectuation involves building connections, putting together commitments from stakeholders, and determining the goals based on who comes on board.

The *lemonade* principle – If life gives you lemons, make lemonade.

The *pilot-in-the-plane* principle – Effectuation recognises human agency as the prime driver of opportunity so the venture should not always stay on a pre-determined path and the entrepreneur can, and should, create opportunities and steer the venture accordingly.[7]

In musical terms a causal approach can be observed in classical music, for which the musicians follow a pre-determined score to cause the piece as already composed to happen, whereas jazz is much more effectual: there isn't a detailed score and, although the musicians follow an agreed theme, in their actual playing they react to opportunities for variations created by what the others do. Effectuation is thus about responding to possibilities as and when they are revealed and developed – rather than causation, which fixes on a method or route in advance and tries to follow it. Causation therefore assumes that the future,

> and therefore a way though it, can to some extent be predicted in advance, whereas effectuation is about exploring what is possible in an uncertain situation where detailed prediction, and therefore reliable preplanning, is not possible.
>
> While the effectuation method may have been formulated by Sarasvathy from her research into people who had started businesses, it is not limited to the business field. It has a much wider application. Indeed Sarasvathy herself, together with Sankaran Venkataraman, has suggested that the 'entrepreneurial method' which follows effectuation principles, should not be thought of as a subdiscipline of economics, management or business studies, but should instead be viewed as having an application analogous to that of the scientific method.[8]

## LOOKING AT WHAT IS ACTUALLY NEEDED

The concept of effectuation is thus based on how entrepreneurs actually operate rather than how it was thought they ought to operate. Also the principles of effectuation do appear to have a much wider application potentially being relevant to all new ventures even in non-business situations.

Effectuation starts with the situation as it is, and with where you are and what is available, instead of starting from where you would like to be in order to achieve a pre-selected final result. It also suggests some other very relevant principles which are not in a standard business plan approach, such as not committing to a new venture more than you can afford to lose and not exclusively determining your route in advance but keeping your eyes open for opportunities as you proceed.

Consistent with the philosophy of effectuation, it is therefore relevant to consider what new ventures are like in reality and what they need, rather than what business theory suggests they should be like and what they should need. The previous section suggested that, as Penrose had pointed out, small businesses are not small big businesses and that new ventures are not necessarily even small businesses. So we should not automatically switch on big-business-based thinking when we think of start-ups because we think of them as embryo businesses. But if they are not small big businesses, and not necessarily embryo businesses at all, what are they?

Start-ups are ventures into the unknown, or at least into an uncertain future which, despite the apparent claims of market research, cannot reliably be predicted. New venturers think that in the unknown there is likely to be something valuable to themselves and/or others and want to find and develop it. Their resources are limited, but they do at least have a sense of adventure or purpose which gives them the drive needed to seek out the opportunity.

That analysis suggests that start-ups have a lot in common with explorers. They too are looking for something in an area which is unexplored, uncertain and not thoroughly mapped, where they cannot be certain that they will find what they want but are willing to make a start with the resources available and to look for promising leads and examine any they find. What they are looking for may be minerals – gold has often been a favourite – or a new route to a particular destination, but they cannot be sure in advance where it is so they need to explore where it seems that it is likely to be found – and they have to do that with the resources available to them.

This book suggests that the analogy between start-up and exploration is a valid one – that people starting a new venture have a lot in common with explorers and relatively little in common with big business managers. That suggests that many of the principles of successful exploration might usefully be applied to start-ups and be a basis for some useful guidance – and that is also consistent with an effectuation approach. Thus this exploration analogy is itself explored in the next chapter.

---

Summary of the Key Points of Chapter 4

- There are other guides available for some types of venture or parts of the start-up process – but many have somewhat limited application.

- Observations of how successful entrepreneurs actually operate have led to the identification of the principles of effectuation – which does seem to be appropriate and to have wider relevance.

- Considerations of the nature of new start-up ventures suggest that, instead of being seen as small big businesses, they have a lot in common with exploration and therefore that the principles guiding successful exploration may also be relevant to start-ups.

# 5
# Enterprise and Exploration

> The Essence of This Chapter
>
> - New start-up ventures should not be seen as small big businesses.
> - Explorations and new venture start-ups have a lot in common and an analogy with exploration does appear to be relevant to start-ups and consistent with effectuation.
> - The very social nature of human behaviour is an important part of the context of new venture exploration.

## THE NATURE OF EXPLORATION

Despite the apparent universal endorsement of the business plan, its hegemony is now being challenged. Among the reasons for this are a reassertion that small businesses are not small big businesses and an increasing realisation that business plans do not actually help small businesses. Other guides to start-up are available – albeit often only for some types of venture or for parts of the start-up process – and the principles of effectuation have been identified from observations of how successful entrepreneurs actually operate.

Further consideration of the nature of start-up ventures suggests that, rather than behaving like small big businesses, they have a lot in common with exploration, for which effectuation is also often appropriate. Therefore the idea of new ventures as a form of exploration is considered further in this section.

Illustration 5.1   Christopher Columbus: Explorer or entrepreneur?

> Christopher Columbus (to use the Anglicised version of his name) was born in Genoa in 1451. He made his living as a sailor and claimed that he first went to sea as early as the age of ten. He acted as an agent on behalf of Genoese and then Portuguese interests and, for them, sailed in the Mediterranean and along the European and African Atlantic coasts. It is recorded that he learned Latin as well as Portuguese and Castilian and read widely about astronomy, geography and history.
> 
> For a long time until the middle of the fifteenth century, Europe had relatively easy access to the Silk Road – the land route to China and India and their valuable goods. But when Constantinople fell to the Turks in 1453, access to Asia and its markets became much more difficult. Columbus, in common with many educated Europeans, understood that the Earth was round and therefore that it should in theory be possible to reach Asia by travelling west. Columbus was also aware of calculations of the size of the Earth and appears to have concluded

that the distance west from the Canary Isles to Japan was only about 3000 Italian miles. That would put it within range of the sailing ships then available, especially if they used the trade winds which he had experienced in his Atlantic voyages. Although this estimate of the distance to Japan was incorrect, it persuaded him that the trip should be possible. (Japan is actually about four to five times as far from the Canary Isles as Columbus believed – depending on whether a great circle route is used or not. The error apparently arose because the estimate that Columbus had of the size of the Earth was too small – possibly because different countries used miles of different lengths – and the estimate of the length of the eastward journey to Japan too large.)

Knowing that Western European countries were keen to find a better means of accessing Eastern markets and thinking that he had an answer for them, Columbus attempted to raise the support he needed for such a venture. He did manage to line up some private Italian investors, but he needed more. He presented his plans to the King of Portugal, to Genoa and Venice and, through his brother, to the King of England, Henry VII. However, none of those pitches produced anything practical and it was the Catholic Monarchs, Ferdinand and Isabella of Spain, who did eventually agree to provide enough support to let the venture proceed.

The result is well known. Between 1492 and 1504 Columbus made four round trips to the

> Americas, but it is not clear whether, when he died in 1506, he fully accepted that what he had discovered was not Asia but a new continent. He had been promised, if he succeeded, that he would be given the rank of Admiral of the Ocean Sea, that he would be appointed viceroy of any new lands he could claim for Spain, and that he would receive a share of the revenues obtained from them. However, his behaviour in the Americas led to complaints, he fell out with the Spanish authorities, and the deal was not implemented as originally intended.

Illustration 5.1 presents a brief history of Christopher Columbus and his achievements. He is probably one of the most famous explorers in history – yet his story is also that of an entrepreneur trying to launch a new venture. In essence he had an idea for a new route to Asian markets which avoided the need to rely on the almost inaccessible silk route – a service for which there was a clear need. His investigation led him to believe that he could deliver that service, but he did not have enough money to do it unaided. Thus he needed to find other backers, which in time he succeeded in doing. The deal he arranged was that, if they put up the money and he found the route, they could use the route and give him a share of the proceeds.

Thus Columbus saw a possible opportunity to enrich himself by developing a service that others needed. To realise this, however, he had to raise sufficient funding from interested investors – a task that proved not to be as easy as he might at first have supposed. But he persevered and eventually he secured the backing he needed and launched his venture. It may be relevant that an account of him is titled *Columbus: His Enterprise* (although it also shows that his was not a record to rejoice in and how he was 'not only obsessed by gold but willing to murder for it'[1] on a horrific scale). However, if his goal was to get to Asia by sailing west, he failed, and, if his goal was to make a lot of money for himself, he also failed. Nevertheless the discovery of the new continent, and in particular its sources of gold, was not unwelcome to his backers and in particular Spain – so they benefited from their investment in his enterprise.

That is a typical story both of an entrepreneur and an explorer and it shows the close connections between new entrepreneurial ventures and explorations. For instance, the things they have in common include:

- They want to do something. They engage in ventures that inevitably have an element of risk, no matter how careful they might be. What are they putting at risk – their lives or livelihoods, their reputations and/or their own investment – and what are the possible rewards likely to justify that risk?

- Both new enterprise venturers and explorers are venturing into the unknown. However much they may try to use existing knowledge to predict what they might encounter, there is a considerable element of uncertainty.

- They need a sense of adventure. Some people may have to try a new business venture because they see no other way of earning a living – and some may be forced to explore because they have been cast out and metaphorically shipwrecked. But generally people do it because they like doing things on their own initiative and/or are willing to try to gain the potential rewards despite the risk involved.

- They also often need external funding. New ventures and explorations can be costly and those wanting to do it may not be able to fund it themselves – at least not unaided.

- Both explorers and new enterprise venturers are well advised to check that their venture could work before they try it. Columbus needed to check that his ships were capable of sailing the distance he thought would take him to Asia and entrepreneurs need to check that the price they think they can charge for a new product, if it can be developed, will cover the likely production costs.

- However, in both cases the final proof is in the eating. Checking that it *could* work is one thing – seeing if it *will* work is another, and the only way of finding out is to try it to see.

- Both explorers and entrepreneurs need some basic skills, or need to team up with others who do have them. Explorers, for instance, need navigation and survival skills – and entrepreneurs need marketing, production and finance skills.

- Where to start can also be an issue for explorers and venturers. Do you start from where you are or do you try to go to somewhere else first because it looks more attractive?

- However, wherever a start is made, it is likely that the most promising opportunities will not be revealed until the journey is under way. So both explorers and venturers would benefit from continuing to look for better opportunities to go in the direction selected, and being ready to respond to such opportunities, instead of just continuing blindly to follow the first apparent route they happen to select.

- For both explorers and venturers, getting started is an important step. It is the moment of commitment that is essential if the goal is to be attained. Before starting there is always an issue of whether more preparation would be beneficial. Once started the decision is made and the incentive is then to keep going because to give up would be to admit failure.

Thus explorers and entrepreneurs do have a lot in common. They are both venturing into the unknown – and should proceed accordingly. To help they both need appropriate skills, they need to get started and to keep going, and they need to be open to any new opportunities that may be revealed throughout the course of the journey.

Illustration 5.2  Explorers and maps

A reflection may be relevant on which comes first – the explorer or the map. Geographic explorers, such as Christopher Columbus, do not explore from maps. Columbus may have had the idea that Japan lay somewhere on the other side of the Atlantic, but if he had had a map of the Atlantic Ocean he would not have needed to explore it. He would have been able to see from the map what was on the other side – and that it wasn't Japan. Columbus had to explore because a realistic map of that part of the world had not been developed – and it was because of the explorations of Columbus and his successors that such maps could later be produced.

To have a map of an area it has to be explored and surveyed first – and the same is the case with new enterprise venturers. They too are venturing into the unknown and the uncertain. Some suggest that prior research can reduce the uncertainty, but reports such as those summarised in Illustration 3.3 indicate that that is not so and that the only way to find out is to go there and test it – in other words to explore it.

Thus the necessity to explore the unknown is another thing that explorers and venturers have in common – and it suggests another reason why business plans are not appropriate for many new ventures. Business plans have been described as route maps for new ventures. In the words of one author: 'the business plan is just like a road map and the planning process is just like map reading'.[2] This assumes that a map is available but you can't have a map for something that has not yet been explored. Realistic maps can be produced later, once the exploration has been done, but they cannot be produced and used before that. (See also Illustration 14.1, p. 135)

## THE NATURE OF THE TERRITORY BEING EXPLORED

If the analogy with exploration is helpful then it may also be relevant to consider the nature of the territory being explored – because that too might indicate some relevant considerations. New ventures are generally being pursued in an environment where the main features with which the explorer is interacting are not mountains or deserts, rivers or jungles, plants or wild animals, but human beings and their activities. New ventures are usually conducted in a milieu of human relationships – with suppliers and customers, colleagues and competitors, funders and supporters. But the real nature of human social behaviour has generally been ignored by many studies of business and economics.

Daniel Kahneman won the Nobel Prize for economics in 2002 for his work on what is referred to as 'behavioural economics', which might be said to recognise how people actually behave as human beings rather than as the logical self-interested calculators that economic theory supposes them to be (see also under Further Information). Kahneman is not an economist but a psychologist who 'became intrigued by the list of assumptions traditional economics made, and still makes, about people's nature'. As Kahneman put it in the 2003 *American Economic Review*, 'I found the list quite startling, because [as a psychologist] I had been professionally trained not to believe a word of it'.[3]

John Kenneth Galbraith, as quoted in Chapter 3, said that 'economic and social behavior are complex'[4] and behavioural economics is starting to recognise the social nature of much of human economic behaviour. As Mark Earls in his book *Herd* comments:

> The influence of others is to be found in every aspect of our lives, in the big and the small things we do. We cannot escape it; even if we pretend we are superior and highly principled and self-determining, we all do it all of the time. We are Super Social Apes.[5]

Earls also adds that an important lesson is that:

> Mass behaviour is inherently complex because it is based on the interaction of individual agents. But we try to understand it as if it were complicated (i.e. reducible to individual component parts). This is why we find it difficult to understand mass behaviour.[6]

The distinction between complex and complicated is similar to the distinction made by Sir Karl Popper between clocks and clouds (see Illustration 5.3). It could be said that a business plan approach assumes that businesses fall into the clock category because it seeks to understand and guide businesses through an analysis of their component parts. Business professionals have constructed their perspective based on this approach, which may be very relevant in theory – at least for big businesses – but, as has been pointed out already, small businesses do not behave in the same way. They are unpredictable, irregular, dynamic and changing. Thus they are much more cloud-like.

Illustration 5.3   Clock or Cloud? Analysing something through its component parts

> According to David Brooks 'through most of human history, people have tried to understand their world through reductive reasoning. That is to say, they have been inclined to take things apart to see how they work'.[7] The assumption is that, even for complicated things, once we understand the parts, it will be easier to work out the behaviour of the whole.
>
> However, Jonah Lehrer has pointed out the problems in such a reductive approach using Sir Karl Popper's distinctions between clocks and clouds.[8] Clocks, he suggested, are predictable and can be understood using reductive methodologies by taking them to pieces to see how the parts interact. Clouds, however, cannot be understood as the sum of their parts; they are unpredictable, irregular and dynamic, changing from second to second. They can best be described through narrative, not numbers. In other words it could be said that the behaviour of clouds is complex.
>
> Popper originally introduced the analogy to make a point about the direction science had taken since the days of Newton. Newton's brilliance showed how the motions of the planets could be predicted with clock-like precision from a few simple physical laws, and that led to what Popper referred to as 'physical determinism' which 'became the ruling faith among enlightened men – assuming that the behaviour of a system could be predicted from the predictable

> behaviour of its components. But, said Popper, it doesn't work, 'physical determinism is a nightmare' and it 'destroys, in particular, the idea of creativity'. Jonah Lehrer, referring to the clock and cloud analogy, also gave it as his opinion that 'we live in a universe, not of clocks, but of clouds'.[9]

Thus behavioural economics, Earls in his examination of human social behaviour, and Popper's clocks and clouds analogy are three examples that all recognise that humans are very significantly influenced, more than they often consciously realise, by social interactions with other human beings. Small businesses, which very much reflect the behaviour and inclinations of their owner-managers, are also affected in this way and behave more like part of a human cloud than components of a clock. Actually it is not just small businesses that are cloud-like. The assumption may be that big businesses behave in a clock-like way, but the evidence is that they too exhibit cloud-like behaviour. That is because they are subject to the same market forces, which come from those people with whom they interact either in other businesses or as individuals – and those people often exhibit mass or herd behaviour. The complex mass behaviour referred to by Earls is exemplified in the movement of flocks of birds, which can indeed seem very cloud-like. Analysis of such flocks suggests that the birds in them don't respond to one leader but to an awareness of what the other birds in the nearby part of the flock are doing. Thus the relationships between the various birds are what matters – and that reinforces the relevance of 'social' contact when working such cloud-like situations.

Therefore it is suggested that clock or cloud considerations support the emphasis placed by behavioural economics on the importance, in business and other contexts, of the social aspect of human nature. The implication for new venturers is that what has been called 'social capital' matters. Successful explorers in this field will need to be aware of and to use the relationships that comprise social capital.

---

Summary of the Key Points of Chapter 5

- Exploration has a lot in common with entrepreneurship and new venture start-ups.

- An analogy with exploration does thus appear to be relevant to start-ups.

- Exploration is necessary because maps do not exist and viable routes cannot be determined in advance. Such consideration helps to explain why realistic and helpful business plans cannot be prepared to guide new ventures.

- The context of exploration also needs to be considered. Many new ventures operate in a human social setting – which means that social capital can be very important.

# 6
# A Guide for Explorers?

> The Essence of This Chapter
> 
> - Maps and pre-prepared route instructions are not available, or appropriate, to guide explorers.
> 
> - Instead, for new venture explorers, a set of guidance principles is offered, based on the earlier analysis.
> 
> - This chapter then lists the principles which are expounded and developed further in Part II.

## EXTRACTING SOME PRINCIPLES

If it is too early for maps, what guidance can be given to explorers? Although it is not practical to advise on what route they should follow, because that needs a map, explorers can be given advice on how best to explore – on how to maximise their chances of a successful outcome while minimising the risks involved.

The principles of effectuation (see Illustration 4.4, p. 45) provide some guidance for new enterprise explorers. The list of features common to both explorers and new enterprise venturers also suggests areas in which such guidance might be helpful. Combining these sources and some of the other issues discussed in the preceding chapters could therefore produce a list of guidance principles for explorers and in particular for new venturers.

Many different lists of such principles are possible. However, with a bias towards venturers, this book selects the following as the ten key ones:

1. Remember that an enterprise is a goal-realisation device – so only engage in a venture if it could help you to achieve your goal(s).

2. Don't commit more than you can afford to lose – and if more is needed find it in other ways.

3. Start from where you are – build on what you have and are.

4. Carry out reality checks and plans – don't be foolhardy and do make some basic checks first.

5. The only reliable test is a real one – the only way you will really know if something new works is to try it.

6. Get started and get some momentum – too much hesitation can kill a venture and, once started, you will have more incentive to keep going and not to fail.

7. Accept uncertainty (and respond to the unforeseen) – if you can't remove the uncertainty, then accept it and act accordingly.

8. Look for opportunities and respond to what you find (be open to opportunities) – because many useful opportunities are only revealed by getting started to see what, and who, is out there.

9. Build, and use, relevant social capital – when working in a human environment human contacts are vital. So know how to build and use them.

10. Acquire the relevant skills (financial but also marketing/sales and production) or find a partner with them – some skills are essential so make sure you have access to them somehow.

If an eleventh principle were to be added it would probably be 'don't try to produce a business plan – unless, and until, it is required or appropriate'. For instance sometimes it may be necessary to produce one because a potential funder requires it, and in such circumstances it makes sense to produce one in order to secure the funding – rather than because it otherwise helps the business. It is also relevant to point out that this list of principles is not a plan: it is not a list of priorities or of sequential stages to be followed in order starting with the first.

Instead they are a set of principles to guide actions as and when they are appropriate and relevant. They do, of course, merit further explanation – and that is provided in Part II.

## PART I RECAPITULATION

If you are thinking of starting a new enterprise then it seems that most official sources of advice will assume both that your new venture is going to be a business and that a business plan is an essential initial requirement for any business. It is as if the business plan is the only tool available for helping anyone to start a venture – but that is not the case.

It has been suggested that the business plan was invented by bankers or, if not, by accountants or other business professionals.[1] Clearly it is widely advocated by people who are professionally involved in advising, training and/or supporting businesses, such as academics, accountants, bankers, consultants, business mentors and people in support agencies, and they find that business plans help their purposes. It also seems likely that the business understanding of many of these professionals has been influenced by a big-business view in which the workings of a business are understood through its component functions. These functions include things like operations and production, selling and marketing, finance, and human resources, which, in a big business, are often undertaken by separate departments. Business schools also teach these component functions of a business as separate business disciplines, thus reinforcing the view that businesses are best understood that way.

Seeing a business as the assembly of its separate functions encourages a functional approach to business analysis and planning. This approach, which can lead to disjointed business thinking, appears to have started with conclusions about big businesses that, it is assumed, can then also be applied to smaller entrepreneurial ventures. The current interest in enterprise and entrepreneurship have grown because they are supposed to lead to people starting businesses, which are seen by governments and others as a key source of net new jobs – and those businesses and jobs are needed to reduce unemployment and provide a foundation for economic growth. Thus enterprise and entrepreneurship have been viewed as a subset of business and, despite what has been said to the contrary, small businesses are often still thought to behave like big businesses, only in a smaller way. Consequently it has become widely accepted that, if small businesses are also businesses, the same methods must work for them and, if big businesses need business plans, small businesses must need them also.

However, the hegemony of the business plan is now being challenged. Other approaches such as effectuation have been identified and this book suggests that new enterprise start-ups also have a lot in common with exploration. Therefore, from such sources, it suggests a set of ten principles to guide new venture start-ups and the explorers running them. These principles are expounded and developed further in Part II.

---

Summary of the Key Points of Chapter 6

- Maps, and pre-prepared route instructions, are not available to guide explorers.

- Instead of maps, a set of ten guidance principles is offered. These are developed further in Part II.

# Part II
# The Ten Principles

> Key Learning Objectives
>
> At the end of Part I a set of ten principles is suggested to guide new venture explorers. Part II explains those principles in more detail. From it readers should gain an understanding of:
>
> - How exploring can be a helpful starting point for new ventures.
>
> - How being guided by the ten principles can help new venture exploring.
>
> - What are the key implications of each of the principles.
>
> - How the principles do not remove the need for entrepreneurial thought, but can help to inform and guide that thinking.

Part I explains that anyone starting a new venture, especially if they describe it as a new business, is likely to be advised that they need to prepare a business plan. That advice is often favoured by accountants, consultants and other business advisers – not least because businesses plans are often helpful to them.

However, their views often appear to be based on big business thinking, which is not necessarily appropriate for small businesses and start-ups. Part I concluded by suggesting that, instead of necessarily being viewed as small big businesses, most new ventures are much better understood as a form of exploring. Therefore a set of new venture exploration principles is suggested to guide them.

Part II explains those principles in more detail, but first, in Chapter 7, it provides a context for them by reviewing the nature of exploration and the exploration aspect of new venturing. This is a book for new venture explorers – people who, instead of being content always to wait for other people to do things first, want to see what they can do themselves to create and/or develop something they think would be helpful. However, what does that exploration involve and what sort of advice can and should usefully be given to those prepared to try it? To try to answer that each of the ten suggested principles is then explained and elaborated in Chapters 8–17. Finally Chapter 18 completes Part II with a brief discussion on how to be guided by the new venture explorer principles.

# 7
# The Starting Point: Understanding How to Explore

> **The Essence of This Chapter**
>
> - To find what they are looking for both explorers and people starting new enterprises have to venture into the unknown.
>
> - When exploring it is not practical to follow a sequential procedure or predetermined path. However, principles can be identified which can guide both explorers and new venturers.
>
> - Understanding the nature of exploration will be helpful in trying to follow those principles.

Explorers suspect and/or hope that what they are looking for is out there to be discovered but they don't know quite where it is or how to go straight to it. Therefore to find it they need to explore, and they don't expect that their first efforts will necessarily succeed and that they will find what they are seeking in the first place they look. New venturers similarly suspect that there is a future for their ideas and they want to find out whether they will work and, if so, what is the best way to make them work – and how to do that without incurring unnecessary and/or unacceptable risk.

Explorers have looked for many things. Columbus looked for a sea route westward to Japan and Amundsen first navigated the Northwest Passage. Speke and Burton looked for the source of the Nile and Scott raced Amundsen to the South Pole. Others sought land routes across America and Australia or new lands on the way in which to settle. Those explorers who are sometimes called prospectors have sought minerals, including particularly gold and, more recently, oil.

What might an explorer want to know? What does exploration involve and what are the relevant issues likely to be? Explorers may be exploring new territory and new venturers may be looking for other things, such as different ways of doings things and different business opportunities in new markets or products. But they and other explorers are all venturing into the uncertain. Because they cannot be sure what it will be like until they try it, they cannot determine in advance precisely what they will find and how they will find it. Thus a step-by-step guide of what to do is not going to work. Instead they need to be able to respond appropriately to the situation as it evolves – so following principles is likely to be much better than trying to follow a sequential guide.

In trying to follow the principles, understanding how to explore will be helpful. Exploring is about venturing into the unknown and the uncertain. It is about trying to discover what is actually there and what things are actually like – things you may suspect exist but can't be sure about. It's about finding what works and what doesn't (often so that it can be eliminated in the search for what does work). Obviously explorers don't want to waste all their time on unproductive effort finding dead ends or things that don't work – so they will try to start with what seems to be the most likely approach. But they realise that they are unlikely to find what they are

# The Starting Point: Understanding how to Explore

looking for immediately and that, in order to be reasonably certain that they ultimately choose a good way, they need to have looked at some of the alternatives as well. Exploring is thus the antithesis of route planning/selection from a map. In order to be able to show all the possible routes on a map it is necessary to explore and survey the territory first – and it is necessary to survey all the territory, whether productive or not, in order to produce a complete map. But explorers do not necessarily need to do that – they just need to find the best route or destination suitable for their purposes. If a map exists then it would be sensible to use it, but even then it may not indicate which route is best for them. So, when no map is available and/or when no suitable route can reliably be identified in advance, it will be necessary to explore.

Illustration 7.1   But which way is best for you?

The principles that follow are designed to help and guide that process. They could be said to start at the beginning – with why someone might want to launch a new venture. Some people may want to explore from a sense of excitement or of restlessness in life. It may only be older readers who will have any recollection of Lee Marvin's rendition of 'I Was Born Under a Wandering Star' from *Paint Your Wagon* – but it exemplifies the venturer who can't settle and soon moves on, leaving others to appreciate the benefits of what he or she has found or developed. Thus people's ultimate exploration goals will vary. They might be trying to see what is there or trying to find something specific, wanting to derive fame and/or fortune from exploration success, or just wanting to experience the excitement or the independence of exploring for themselves.

Then there is the issue of where to start. The stereotypical Irish advice to someone seeking directions is reputed to be 'I wouldn't start from here', but, lacking teleporting machines or the equivalent, most explorers have to start from where they are – and with what they have. They might wish it were otherwise but they would be well advised to explore within the limits, but also *to* the limits, of their own abilities and the resources they have or can find.

What then are the things that have to be done to progress the exploration? For the new enterprise explorer they will include developing the product or service to be provided, developing and securing customers for it, putting in place the necessary venture infrastructure and managing the finances that pay for, or flow from, all of that. Thus a range of different skills will be needed and they have to be learnt or otherwise acquired.

Another important aspect of making progress is knowing how best to operate in conditions of uncertainty. Given the options of accepting that uncertainty or trying to reduce it, some might think it is sensible to try to reduce uncertainty by prior research – and that indeed is what the business plan approach tries to do. However, others now recognise that, while it is still sensible to look ahead as far as is possible, many attempts to predict the future are unreliable and that trying to remove all uncertainty in this way is a false hope (see Illustration 3.3). Therefore it is sensible to accept that there will be uncertainty and to proceed accordingly. That can mean expecting that the unexpected can happen – and so looking for, and being ready to respond to, problems and, very importantly, opportunities, if and when they are revealed.

But because a new venture is necessarily operating in conditions of uncertainty, the downside is the risk that it doesn't work. Ultimately failure can't be ruled out – and so should be allowed for in a sensible explorer's approach. What is the explorer ultimately willing to sacrifice – does it go as far as life and limb, or even just the equivalent of a limb? Thus, however much a new venture explorer wants to be proved right, it is important to ask questions about whether the methods are working and whether there might be better ways of doing things.

Two particular things that are often of crucial relevance to the new venture explorer, but which do not seem to form part of any standard business plan, are momentum and social capital. These relate to the psychological boost that activity and progression can provide once the venture has got started and the fact that human beings are very socially influenced and any new enterprise venture will operate in that social context.

And a final comment – not a principle of exploring as such, but nevertheless relevant for new enterprise explorers: don't do a business plan unless, and until, you have to.

So the successful new venture explorer is likely to be someone who:

1. Knows what he or she is looking for ultimately.

2. Does not commit so much to the venture that, if the first part is not immediately productive, they are then stranded. (They need to have at least enough in reserve to be able to get back.)

3. Starts from where they are.

4. Thinks about and plans their approach – and checks that it could work.

5. But nevertheless realises that, however much they suspect something is there, the only reliable test is a real one and no amount of prior assessment can remove the uncertainty.

6. Sees the benefit in getting started and getting some momentum – because too much hesitation can kill a venture and, once started, they will have more incentive to keep going.

7. Accepts uncertainty (and responds to the unforeseen) – if they can't remove the uncertainty they accept it, and act accordingly.

8. Continues to look for opportunities and responds to what is found (is open to opportunities) – because

## The Starting Point: Understanding how to Explore

many useful opportunities are only revealed by getting started to see what and who is out there.

9. Knows that, when working in a human environment, social contacts are vital – so they build, and use, relevant social capital.

10. Acquires the relevant skills (financial but also marketing/sales and production) or finds a partner with them – some skills are essential so make sure you have access to them somehow.

Illustration 7.2   Explorers often don't get it right the first time – but that isn't failure

> Explorers don't expect that their first efforts will succeed and that they will automatically find what they are looking for in the first place they look. That is why they need to explore. So don't needlessly see failure where it doesn't exist. Instead, recognise that finding dead ends or things which don't work is an essential part of exploring because such discoveries are important steps on a path to eventual success.
>
> It is reported that, when he was trying to find something that would serve as a reliable filament for electric light bulbs, Edison found that none of the first groups of things he tried were suitable. However, instead of seeing this as failure, Edison reputedly saw it as progress:
>
>> If I find 10,000 ways something won't work, I haven't failed. I am not discouraged,

because every wrong attempt discarded is often a step forward.[1]

I would construct and work along various lines until I found them untenable. When one theory was discarded, I developed another at once. I realized very early that this was the only possible way for me to work out all the problems.[2]

Thus for an explorer finding that something doesn't work is not necessarily failure. It has added information about where not to look further. Nevertheless, how many people either class that as failure or alternatively continue to try the same thing hoping for a different result?

---

Summary of the Key Points of Chapter 7

- Both exploring and starting a new enterprise involve venturing into the unknown.

- Because it is venturing into the unknown, it is not practical to plan a detailed route in advance. However, principles can be identified that can guide both explorers and new venturers.

- These principles are likely to be more helpful if those trying to follow them understand the nature of exploration.

# 8

# Principle 1 – An Enterprise Is a Means, Not an End

> **The Essence of This Chapter**
>
> - An enterprise is a means not an end.
>
> - Therefore anyone considering a venture should identify their aim(s) and only engage in an enterprise if it is likely to help them to achieve those aims.
>
> - However, immediate concerns may not be the same thing as longer-term aims.

Part I quotes the comment that 'an enterprise is a goal-realisation device'[1]: a remark that helps to highlight the principle that an enterprise is a means not an end. This principle is about considering the ends before focussing on the means – and then not forgetting the goal in the excitement and pressure that the means involve. So, before you engage in a new venture, it is important to consider whether it will help you to achieve your goal(s) and, once it is under way and consuming a lot of energy, it is important not to be so obsessed with the challenge that you forget why you are doing it. Without knowing where the goalposts are it is hard to know where to position yourself on the pitch or in which direction to play the ball.

So why would someone want to start a new venture? It might be expected that many people would do it for the money, but money is itself a means to an end and people want money because they want things that money can buy, such as food and housing, or entertainment and pleasure. Thus, while many people might want some money from their venture, not least because otherwise they could not afford to do it, money is not the ultimate purpose and is itself a means to an end – and Table 8.1 lists some other possible goals.

Table 8.1 *Possible goals*

Most people have to work in some way, but they might do so for a variety of goals. The list below includes some possibilities, many of which people can realise through having their own enterprise. But the enterprise itself is not the goal, it is just a means to that end.

- To make a contribution to society and to other people.
- To discover something, for instance in science or exploration.
- To create art and/or to express themselves through art.
- To be famous and/or to have status.
- To make a fortune.
- To be respected and to have influence.
- To achieve success in sport, or in other activities.
- To belong to a group or community.
- To have a secure future and retirement.
- To raise a family.
- To obtain pleasure and gratification.
- To survive.

This list has a lot in common with Maslow's hierarchy of needs (see Figure 8.1) in which the lower order needs predominate until they are addressed and higher order needs are only perceived once lower order needs have been satisfied. Note that money does not feature in Malsow's list of needs – for the reasons already indicated.

It is easier to use money to buy things lower down on the list in Table 8.1 (and in Maslow's hierarchy) than those towards the top. Everyone needs resources for things like survival and raising a family. Some people are fortunate enough to inherit, win or marry significant amounts of money, and can use that money to satisfy those needs. For everyone else, however, satisfying their needs requires the expenditure of effort in some form, a process often referred to as work. Even those with money have to work at things like esteem and self-actualisation, although having money can give people more time or inclination to concentrate on

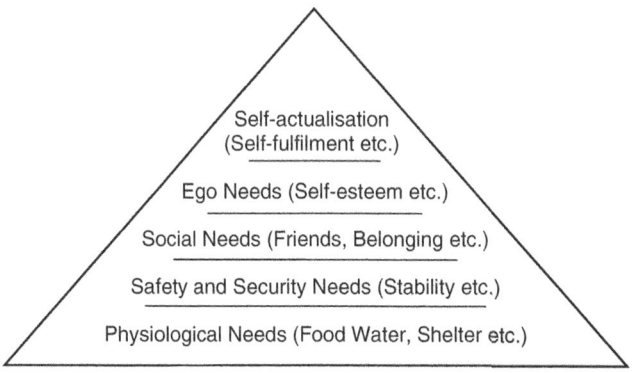

Figure 8.1 *Maslow's hierarchy of needs*

Source: Based on A. H. Maslow, 'A Theory of Human Motivation', *Psychological Review* 50/4, (1943) pp. 370–96.

self-actualisation because they do not have to worry about earning enough to feed or house themselves.

Thus the reasons people might want to engage in a new venture are similar to the reasons they might want to work. They can include being able to enjoy pleasurable activities, trying to live and raise a family, wanting to make a contribution to society and to other people, trying to discover something or create a new piece of art, or to gain respect or influence. For that they need resources and money is often the means they use to get those resources (but see Table 8.2). It is rare that money itself is the goal – unless they see the amount of money they have as some sort of score for how well they are doing in their lives.

Maslow's hierarchy is a useful reminder that the important goals may not be the obvious ones. As has been said: when you are up to your knees in alligators

Table 8.2 *Other ways to find resources*

- Acquire a pension or annuity
- Beg, or live off friends or relatives
- Crime
- Get a job
- Hunter-gathering or self-sufficient farming
- Inherit wealth
- Marry wealth
- Sponsorship
- Unemployment or invalidity benefit payments
- Win the lottery

*Source*: Based on S. Bridge, *Rethinking Enterprise Policy* (Basingstoke: Palgrave Macmillan, 2010) p. 153.

## Principle 1 – An Enterprise is a Means, not an End

it is easy to forget that your aim was actually to drain the swamp. When lower order needs are pressing it is easy to forget higher order ones and similarly, in specifying objectives, it is easy to set short-term targets while overlooking the underlying but longer-term aim.

An example of where a failure to recognise the real aim led to a missed opportunity is related by John Masters. He recounts that as an army officer, while at staff college, he was told that in 1935 both the (British) Army and the Royal Air Force wanted to improve their ability to detect enemy aircraft beyond the distance that the existing searchlights and sound rangers could then manage. Each service gave the scientific establishment a target to be achieved. The Army said they wanted searchlights and sound rangers that could pick up an aircraft at 30,000 feet and 20 miles, instead of the then limit of 20,000 feet and 10 miles, and in due course they got better searchlights and better sound rangers. But, by not thinking through their needs properly, they missed an opportunity. The RAF defined their aim more accurately and said that they wanted to detect and track aircraft from as great a distance as possible. They got radar.[2]

People can have multiple goals, and those goals can, and do, change as their lives progress. Figure 8.2 alludes to some of them and presents them in the context of the unknown territory through which a route to them has to be found. But it is not only possible, but likely, that as the journey progresses the ultimate destination will change.

Therefore, if you want to start a new venture, think about why. What is it you want to get out of it? The goals and benefits sought might include any of the objectives listed in Table 8.3. If you think that you

Figure 8.2  *What are an individual's goals?*

*Source*: S. Bridge, 'Could a Comparison with Medicine Help Our Understanding of Entrepreneurship?' Paper presented at the ISBE 28th National Conference, 2005.

are likely to achieve any, or even all, of them through a new venture then this book is for you. But only engage in a venture if it could help you to achieve your goal(s), so do check that – because a venture that is not going to get you what you want is unlikely to be helpful.

Table 8.3 *Possible reasons for launching a new venture*

*Possible goals:*

To do something for yourself.

To do something for your team, group, community (including yourself).

To do something for others.

*Possible benefits:*

The excitement of doing it.

A sense of achievement.

An expected output – for instance money, discovery, achievement and/or fame.

An unexpected output – which was not anticipated but is nevertheless welcome.

## A Note on Terminology

This chapter, and the rest of this book, refers variously to enterprises, ventures and businesses. Often books for or about start-ups assume that they are describing start-up businesses and therefore refer to them all as businesses. If, by business, that means a private sector organisation (or social enterprise) that seeks to make a financial profit to distribute (or surplus to reinvest) from its activities, then clearly some new ventures are not businesses. In any case, referring to them as businesses encourages people to think of them as businesses and then to apply received business wisdom to them – which is often based on big business methods. In reality, small businesses are not small big businesses, and many new ventures are not even going to be small businesses. Therefore, by referring to them as ventures, this book seeks to avoid the assumption that 'business' thinking should automatically be applied. Instead, ventures are enterprises that might, or might not, later become a business – and in such contexts the word 'enterprise' is also used, either to avoid over-use of the word venture or to indicate that the people behind the new ventures are being enterprising. (For more on the terminology see Illustration 1.2 and 'new venture terminology' in the Further Information section.)

---

Summary of the Key Points of Chapter 8

- An enterprise is not an end in itself, but it may be a means to an end.

- Therefore, before starting a new enterprise, venturers should consider whether it is likely to help them to achieve their aim(s).

- In deciding what the aims are it is important to look behind immediate concerns to identify longer-term objectives.

# 9
# Principle 2 – Don't Commit More than You Can Afford to Lose

> **The Essence of This Chapter**
>
> - The future is uncertain and enterprise involves risk. It is therefore possible that at some stage an enterprise may not work.
>
> - So do not invest in an enterprise more than you can afford to lose. Then you will be able to continue if your exploration fails at some stage.
>
> - If the enterprise needs more than you can afford, learn how to find it in other ways.

Consider the downside risk and don't at any stage commit to an uncertain venture more than you can afford to lose. The future is uncertain and, in any case, it has been said that enterprise is spelt R-I-S-K. Some people try to quantify the risk and reduce the uncertainty through market research, but that can be expensive and, as Illustration 3.3 suggests, rarely works. Saras Sarasvathy found that the 'expert' entrepreneurs she interviewed distrusted it and revealed 'a profound distrust of attempts to predict the future'.[1] So, if the element of risk remains, the sensible new venture explorer will plan accordingly.

One aspect of that planning is accepting the possibility that things will not go as hoped and the venture will not succeed. Of course that would be a disappointing outcome, but that disappointment would be a disaster if the new venture explorer had invested so much in the venture that they are then ruined. Therefore, as Sarasvathy found, her experts were not prepared to invest more than they could afford to lose. They were at least prepared for the possibility that this time it might not work.

Principles are not inviolable laws – they can be ignored – but they are still sensible advice, and this principle is no different. This is what sensible explorers did. They left enough in reserve so that they could get back if they didn't find what they were looking for. Naturally some of them ignored this principle and literally or figuratively burnt their boats and committed themselves, in effect, to succeeding or dying in the attempt. Some were lucky and did succeed, but others became stranded and died as a result. Nevertheless the sensible ones did not go that far and ensured that, if the current attempt did not succeed they had a good chance of surviving to try again when they perceived the conditions to be more favourable.

In essence therefore this principle is about how you should resource your new venture. By all means commit yourself to the venture, but not to the extent that, if it fails, as it might, you will then be ruined. In other words do not invest more than you can afford to lose. However, this requires a different way of thinking to that traditionally advocated, at least for businesses.

The traditional, or causal, way was to ascertain how much money was needed and then to try to find it. How much is needed is thus determined by the nature of the venture and was usually ascertained by means of a business plan. It was considered that whatever the business plan estimated was required was the key amount that must logically be needed to make the venture work – so that was what the new venture explorer should then try to raise.

The effectual way starts, however, not with the venture, but the person. As explained above the principle is that the new venture explorer should not invest more than he or she can afford to lose – so the amount is determined by the person, not the enterprise. However, if the focus is on the venture, it might be argued that this is not enough and the effectual approach will lead to failure because the venture will be under-resourced.

That is why a different way of thinking is required. The causal approach, focussing on the venture to be created, argues for the amount needed, even if it is more than the venturer can afford to lose. The effectual approach looks at it in a different way. It does not deny that the venture, as thus conceived, might require more, but it suggests that if that amount is not affordable, the venture should be approached in a different way. For instance can it be done more cheaply? Is it essential to invest in production capacity initially – or could it be sub-contracted? Can appropriate partners be found, such as suppliers or customers, who stand to gain from the venture and who might invest in it? Thus the venture is built on the means available, not the predetermined result sought (see Principle 3).

One example of an entrepreneur who could not afford to finance his enterprise himself and therefore needed to find other partners in the venture was Columbus (see Illustration 5.1). For a venture like his he needed backing from people who not only could afford to take the risk of backing him but who would also be in a position to capitalise on the results if he was successful. Thus he lobbied various monarchs in Europe and eventually obtained support from King Ferdinand of Aragon and Queen Isabella of Castile (the Catholic Monarchs of Spain). The amount they put at risk was within what they could afford to lose and, although Columbus failed to reach Asia, which was his goal, the colonies he established in America and other conquests in the subsequent decades would lead to an influx of wealth into Spain.

Often the investment that might be put at risk in a venture is thought of in terms of money. But, as well as money, someone considering a new venture is likely also to put in time and reputation. Because of this, the person is likely to put at risk other aspects of their life, such as family relationships. Therefore the principle of not committing more than you can afford to lose applies to these considerations also – not just to the financial aspects.

But what is being put at risk if the venture is not attempted? There are also dangers in not proceeding. Therefore, as well as considering what might be lost if the venture does not work, it can also be relevant to consider what might be forfeit if the venture is not tried. Will there then be a sense of regret for not trying something and for not at least exploring alternatives and seeing if an idea could work? The point of this principle is to find a way to explore those possibilities while not risking disaster if they don't work.

## IN CONCLUSION

The business-plan-based and exploration-based approaches therefore represent two different ways of thinking. Business plans encourage the new venture explorer to commit the investment that the full enterprise seems to need – even if the venturer can't easily afford it. Then, if it doesn't work, the venturer is sunk. But such an investment is never risk-free – so follow the principle of not committing more than you can afford to lose. That might require the adoption of a different perspective, considering how to risk little and fail cheap and, if more is needed, looking for other ways of providing it.

Illustration 9.1 The danger of trusting a business plan – and of putting too much at risk

> One of the authors once interviewed a young woman who, with a partner, had started a fashion clothing business. They had attended a business start-up programme for graduates and appeared to have done well at the beginning – they had attracted a lot of interest and won a prestigious business start competition. After a while, however, they ran out of money and the business collapsed.
> 
> The interview, which was something in the nature of a post mortem, revealed that, while the partners had a business plan, this had been prepared for them largely by an adviser in an effort to help them to win the competition. Further, although the course they had been on had covered financial issues, the partners had

missed the bit that dealt with cash flow projections, as they were away that day for part of the competition. Nevertheless they had believed the plan, which projected that the business would be profitable – after all the advisor who had prepared much of it was one of their tutors and thus supposedly an expert. However, the partners had not understood how the business plan was constructed and they had failed to appreciate the need to keep a close watch on the cash flow and maintain an income stream. As a result they spent money faster than they were receiving it, with the inevitable result.

A further outcome from the failure was that the parents of one of the partners lost their house, which they had mortgaged to provide the venture with the investment that the business plan indicated was both required and justified.

Summary of the Key Points of Chapter 9

- Because the future is uncertain, venturing into it with a new enterprise has an unavoidable element of risk. While a lot may be gained if it works, the new venture explorer should also be prepared for the possibility that the enterprise will not succeed.

- Therefore the important principle to follow is not to invest in an enterprise more than you can afford to lose – in money, time, reputation or other commodity. Then, if the enterprise does fail at some stage, you will still be able to try again or continue to do other things.

- If the enterprise needs more resources than you can afford to invest then look for other ways in which it might be done or other sources of the investment required.

# 10
# Principle 3 – Start from Where You Are

> **The Essence of This Chapter**
>
> - Don't handicap yourself by starting something for which you have to build or acquire everything from scratch – even if the supposed end-product looks exciting.
>
> - Instead build on what you already have: on your ideas, skills, experience and contacts.

Start from where you are and go in the direction you want to go. Like the other principles, following this one is not compulsory – but it is sensible. Successful entrepreneurs often maximise their chances of success by developing ideas in areas in which they have some training and/or knowledge, some experience and some relevant contacts.

It has been said that entrepreneurial success comes from a combination of idea, know-how and know-who[1] and therefore if you choose an idea for which you have little or no relevant know-how (your experience and knowledge and your abilities and skills) and know-who (your contacts) you are effectively increasing your chances of failure.

Starting from where you are is a key principle of effectuation (see Illustration 4.4). In explaining

Table 10.1 *What makes a good idea?*

What makes an idea a good one from which to start a new venture? Some of the considerations might be:
- Is it (relatively) easy to do? Is it likely to be doable with the resource and capabilities available?
- Is there a market with growth potential? Is the market likely to arise from a long-term trend or just a short-term fad?
- Is there a suitable route to market, including a distribution system if appropriate?
- Is there a USP (unique selling proposition) – for instance something protected by a patent or trade secret?
- Is the environment acceptable for the venture? Is it for instance stable or dynamic? And is the venture suitable for the environment and is it ecologically sustainable?
- Is there potential to improve the product/service offering?
- Is there potential to scale up the venture if it works?

Then there are questions to consider about the feasibility of the venture:
- Is the idea doable – by someone?
- Is it doable by you? Can you do it? Do you (and your entrepreneurial team) have the requisite competency and commitment (including time and emotional commitment) and perhaps related to what you can afford to lose)?
- Is it worth doing? Financially – what are the downsides, what are the risks, and what are the potential rewards? Can you resource it? Can you resource it personally, can you ask friends or family to invest, or are you seeking a serious contribution from outsiders?
- Do you want to do it? Does it help you to achieve your goal?

## Principle 3 – Start From Where You Are

the contrasting concepts of causation and effectuation, Saras Sarasvathy has suggested that causation is the approach of a cook who, in order to prepare a meal, first decides on what dish to cook, then looks up a recipe, assembles the listed ingredients and follows the recipe to prepare the dish initially chosen. Effectuation, on the other hand, she suggests would be to start to prepare a meal, not by selecting a target dish, but by considering the ingredients available and then deciding how they might be put together to create a dish, based on the abilities and ideas of the chef.

Both approaches actually depend on the ability of the chef to produce an acceptable result, and neither will guarantee success. Also, many cooks will sometimes use one approach and sometime the other. Usually they will work with what is in season and available, but sometimes, possibly on special occasions, they will select a particular recipe and then go to the bother of searching out the specific ingredients needed – or they may even mix the two approaches by selecting a recipe but adapting it to some extent to the ingredients more easily to hand or to suit consumer preferences.

Cooking what you can cook with what you've got is described by Sarasvathy as the bird-in-the-hand approach. You know what ingredients you have and they are likely to be ingredients that you know how to use – whereas trying to do something special with unfamiliar ingredients may potentially offer a more attractive result but is much more risky. Starting from where you are and with what you know and what you have is sensible in terms of issues such as cost and ability to deliver. Basing your venture on the ideas, experiences, skills and contacts you already have is

Table 10.2 *Comparison of goal-focussed and means-driven approaches*

| Goal-focussed (causal) | Means-driven (effectual) |
| --- | --- |
| Encourages you to launch a venture based on a predetermined concept of the idea that you want to realise. | Encourages you to launch a venture based on your experience, contacts and what you can do – and to see what you can construct from that. |
| Encourages you to follow a business planning process to determine how much money will be needed to start the venture, and then to try to find it, however much it is. | Encourages you to base your venture on no more resource than you can afford to lose – plus on what you can get other partners to contribute. |
| Keeps your eyes focused narrowly on achieving the goal by your chosen route. | Keep looking broadly in case there are better opportunities to take you in the direction in which you want to go. |
| Acute awareness of your weaknesses – don't start until these are improved. | Acute awareness of your strengths – and don't worry too much about your weaknesses but look for ways round them. |
| Once started there is little room for change. | You can change if obstacles, market feedback and/or the appearance of better opportunities suggest that it would be advisable. |
| Encourages you to adapt to fit the target or opportunity. | Encourages you to adapt the opportunity or target to fit your overall goals. |
| If the initial plans do not work out that is perceived to be a failure. | If the first ways tried don't work out that is to be expected in exploration as part of the way to eventual success. |
| Because the goal is fixed, resource-seeking becomes a somewhat barren process. | Because the goal can change to suit the partners who come on board and the opportunities found, resource-seeking can become a constructive and energising process. |

the essence of this principle, because it is more likely to produce an acceptable result than aiming for something apparently attractive but which is beyond your experience and which requires know-how and know-who that you do not possess. Where the future is unknown and there is already a lot of uncertainty the situation will not be helped at all by adding the extra complication of unnecessarily operating beyond your skills and experience.

Thus even if you know you want to do something but are not sure what, the sensible place to start looking for possibilities is from your own skills, experience and contacts – and not by copying others or picking ideas at random just because they seem attractive.

---

Summary of the Key Points of Chapter 10

- Even if the projected end result looks desirable, if you try to do something for which you do not have a lot of relevant experience, skills and/or contacts you will be imposing a big handicap.

- Instead you are much more likely to succeed if you build your venture on what you have already got, on what you have and are, and on your existing ideas, skills, experience and contacts.

# 11

# Principle 4 – Carry Out Reality Checks and Make Appropriate Plans

> The Essence of This Chapter
>
> - Jumping into an exploration with no prior consideration is foolhardy.
>
> - So think about what you are going to do and check that it could work, or at least that there are no obvious reasons why it shouldn't work.
>
> - Then plan and prepare your approach to the venture.

Whereas most of the other principles indicate a general approach, this principle advocates some specific actions. It suggests that before starting a venture you should both check that it could work and plan what you are going to do.

Business plans involve both checks and plans and Part I suggested that they are not helpful – but that is because of the way that checking and planning are done and the way that the business plan is presented as the correct and essential tool to use, not because planning itself is not necessary. This principle advocates that checking and planning are done, but appropriately for the situation and not to excess – and the planning should not be so prescriptive that it can harm the venture.

Illustration 11.1   Checking scientific theories

> In science it is not possible to prove that a theory is correct. Why then, if you have a new theory, would you bother checking it?
> 
> Scientific theories are checked against known facts, not to see if they are right, but to see if they are wrong. If a theory can be shown to be consistent with current knowledge, and is not therefore disproved, then it is accepted as a reasonable working assumption until such time as new findings emerge that show that it is wrong. As it is always presumed to be possible that at some time in the future such findings will emerge, it is never possible to be sure that the theory is right. However, once it is shown that a theory is not consistent with reliable experimental results then it can be declared to be wrong.
> 
> Thus it is a sensible precaution to check a new theory against existing knowledge to see if there is anything which will prove it wrong now and save the effort that will be wasted, and the damage that might be done, if a wrong theory were to be taken further and used as the basis for further work.

In science you can't prove that something will work, but you can check that there do not appear to be any obvious reasons why it shouldn't work before you start to put too much trust in it. In a similar way, when the future is uncertain you can't plan for every eventuality, but it is nevertheless sensible to consider what you are likely to need and to make provision accordingly, rather than starting out with nothing.

Illustration 11.2    Holiday preparation

> When setting off on holiday it is sensible to check that your travel arrangements should get you to your destination – for instance that the flight that you have selected does fly on that day and does go to the right place – and that there are no forecast air traffic controller strikes or typhoons. Then you will need to plan your departure. You will need to consider what clothes you are likely to need, and to pack them. You also need to decide how you are going to travel to the airport and how long that is likely to take, after checking weather and traffic conditions, and, if appropriate, you need to book a taxi and set the alarm accordingly.
> 
> It is probably sensible to plan your trip to the airport based on the assumption that the plane will take off on time, not least because, even if it does take off late, you may still be refused a place on it if you don't check in punctually. However, although many flights are punctual they can be delayed – and disembarkation and immigration and customs processes can take time, so you probably shouldn't assume that you will be able to leave the airport promptly and make further arrangements for onward travel for which a timely arrival is crucial.

For a new enterprise what are the key things to check? First, do the sums add up? Are the resources you think you will generate likely to be enough to cover the costs you think you will incur? Second, do you think you have the capability to do it? Can you put together the necessary production facilities? And third, can you, or someone else, manage the whole process and deliver a working enterprise?

There are, of course, other important issues you might be advised to check, but it is not possible to specify here precisely what to check and to plan – because that will depend on the specific venture. Some possibilities are nevertheless indicated in Table 11.1.

As well as the question of what to check, there is also the issue of what level of checking is appropriate, and what planning should then be done to allow for the eventualities foreseen. For the holiday described in Illustration 11.2 it might be reasonable to check how long the journey to the airport should usually

Table 11.1 *What to check*

---

What to check will depend on the venture but it might include:

- Can you produce it?

- Can you sell it?

- Will the price to be charged cover the production costs incurred?

- What level of sales is necessary at least to break even and is the market likely to be big enough for that?

- Are there any legal or technical restrictions that might prevent you from doing what you want to do?

take, and then to allow a little extra for further minor delays *en route*. But would it be reasonable to travel to the airport the day before, and stay in an airport hotel overnight, just in case there is a major accident on the approach road and it was blocked for hours? Of course there are no right and wrong answers. It is up to you as a new venture explorer to decide how much it is sensible to do to check, as far as you reasonably can, that there are no good reasons why it shouldn't work and that you have allowed for the foreseeable eventualities, and made provision accordingly.

Illustration 11.3   Some prior provision can be helpful for unforeseen eventualities

Summary of the Key Points of Chapter 11

- This principle is about the wisdom of looking before you leap – and, in planning your leap, you need to allow for any obstacles or targets you see.

- Starting an exploration with no prior consideration would be foolhardy.

- So think about what you are going to do and check that there are no obvious reasons why it shouldn't work.

- Then plan and prepare your approach to the venture accordingly.

# 12
# Principle 5 – The Only Reliable Test Is a Real One

> The Essence of This Chapter
>
> - Market research techniques for trying to predict the market's response to a new venture can be costly and are often unreliable.
>
> - The only way to see how people will actually respond to something is to do it for real: offering a real product (or service) in a real situation.

Will your enterprise (idea) work and what is the easiest way to find out reliably? In theory there are two options: either doing it for real or conducting prior market research to try to assess likely reactions and thus reduce the risk that an offering will not work. Market research should thus be the sensible option, but the problem is that often it doesn't work. The only way you will really know if something new works is to try it.

## THE PROBLEM WITH MARKET RESEARCH

In 1985, in response to a perceived preference by young people for the taste of Pepsi, Coca-Cola introduced New Coke. It did this after an extensive programme of market research which had indicated that its new flavour was overwhelmingly preferred by consumers over both Pepsi and traditional Coke. Yet only 77 days later, after an increasingly negative reaction, the old flavour was reintroduced as Coca-Cola Classic. The market research had failed to predict how the market would actually respond. In the case of Baileys Irish Cream, market research also apparently failed to predict how the market would react. In this case, however, the research suggested that the new product would have little appeal, yet it was launched despite that because of a manager's instinctive feeling that it would sell. The result was that the market liked it and Baileys was such a success that it has been copied by other liqueur creams.

As David Ogilvy once put it: 'the trouble with market research is that people don't think how they feel, they don't say what they think and they don't do what they say' – and to that could be added that they don't and can't know how they will react to a new product. As Henry Ford is reputed to have said, 'If I had asked my customers what they wanted, they would have said a faster horse'.

According to Philip Graves 'when market research wanders into the realm of the future it is inherently reckless'.[1] In his book *Consumer.ology* he highlights reasons why asking people whether they would buy something may not produce a reliable answer. Among the suggestions from this and other sources are:

- People don't actually know how they will react. However, they think they do and, because of a compulsion to rationalise, they can instinctively invent rational reasons for what they think they will do and so can provide apparently rational, credible and consistent answers to market research questions (see also Illustration 18.1).

- People want to be logical and/or helpful – and that affects the answers they will give to researchers' questions. They think their decision would be logical and so their answers will be based on that assumption. But in reality, many purchases are made not as a result of logical analysis but under the influence of 'fantasies, feelings and fun'[2] and so what they will actually do is not what they like to think they would do.

- People may not realise it, but their responses will depend on their frame of mind and the circumstances under which they are being asked. Thus the choice they indicate they will make when they are relaxed and sitting comfortably in a focus group discussing a product may be different from the choice they make when short of time in a crowded supermarket.

Some people don't use, or pay heed to, market research. They think that they know the market and so don't need others to assess it for them. In the case of Baileys Irish Cream, events showed that the producers did know their market, but there are also examples where the people it might be supposed should know were wrong. Several successful entrepreneurs will admit to having experienced considerable initial scepticism from bankers, investors, competitors or industry experts. At the beginning of the 1970s IBM and Digital were leaders in the market for computers when all the computers were mainframes. They thought they knew all about the demand for computers, but failed to recognise the possibility for a significant market for personal computers. As the Chairman of Digital said in 1977, 'there is no reason for any individual to have a computer in their home' and thus it was left to others such as Apple to demonstrate that such a market did indeed exist. So apparent industry knowledge and/or instinct can sometimes work, but on other occasions may be as unreliable as other sources of market forecasts.

**Testing It for Real**

This principle acknowledges that much so-called market research doesn't work and that it and a supposed feel for the market are not going to be reliable guides, especially for new offerings. Thus the only way to find out how the market will react is to conduct a test for real. Of course the explorer should do what checking he or she can, provided it is not too costly, but if there is still a feeling that people will buy what it is proposed should be offered, then the only reliable way to test that is by actually offering it.

Illustration 12.1   The coat question

- People want to be logical and/or helpful – and that affects the answers they will give to researchers' questions. They think their decision would be logical and so their answers will be based on that assumption. But in reality, many purchases are made not as a result of logical analysis but under the influence of 'fantasies, feelings and fun'[2] and so what they will actually do is not what they like to think they would do.

- People may not realise it, but their responses will depend on their frame of mind and the circumstances under which they are being asked. Thus the choice they indicate they will make when they are relaxed and sitting comfortably in a focus group discussing a product may be different from the choice they make when short of time in a crowded supermarket.

Some people don't use, or pay heed to, market research. They think that they know the market and so don't need others to assess it for them. In the case of Baileys Irish Cream, events showed that the producers did know their market, but there are also examples where the people it might be supposed should know were wrong. Several successful entrepreneurs will admit to having experienced considerable initial scepticism from bankers, investors, competitors or industry experts. At the beginning of the 1970s IBM and Digital were leaders in the market for computers when all the computers were mainframes. They thought they knew all about the demand for computers, but failed to recognise the possibility for a significant market for personal computers. As the Chairman of Digital said in 1977, 'there is no reason for any individual to have a computer in their home' and thus it was left to others such as Apple to demonstrate that such a market did indeed exist. So apparent industry knowledge and/or instinct can sometimes work, but on other occasions may be as unreliable as other sources of market forecasts.

**Testing It for Real**

This principle acknowledges that much so-called market research doesn't work and that it and a supposed feel for the market are not going to be reliable guides, especially for new offerings. Thus the only way to find out how the market will react is to conduct a test for real. Of course the explorer should do what checking he or she can, provided it is not too costly, but if there is still a feeling that people will buy what it is proposed should be offered, then the only reliable way to test that is by actually offering it.

Illustration 12.1   The coat question

> Have you ever left your home/office and, in getting yourself ready to go, asked the person beside you, 'Do I need a coat?'. You are trying to make a judgement based on your interpretation of the weather from inside the building, not having been outside. However, the only reliable test for evaluating whether or not you need a coat is to go outside and find out. The chances are that the coat will come in useful if it is cold or rainy. However, if the sun shines, the coat soon becomes extra baggage.

Principle 2 suggests that you shouldn't commit more than you can afford to lose, so, if possible, don't go to all the expense of producing a completely finished product and making a big launch before seeking feedback. One way of avoiding that is by starting in a relatively small way until you can see what does work and what is likely to justify further investment. In other words, find your first customers and try it from there. Learn more effectively about the market and identify further opportunities by being in the market, not by trying to 'research' it from outside. (See also Lean Startup in Illustrations 4.3 and 12.2.)

Illustration 12.2   Lean Startup

> Lean Startup is introduced in Illustration 4.3, p. 43. The concept arose from the work of Eric Ries and Steve Blank. Ries had worked in, and for, a number of start-up businesses in Silicon Valley, where Blank

also worked as an entrepreneur and academician. Blank had created the 'Customer Development' methodology in the 1990s and Ries was at one time his student: 'the best student I ever had'.

Customer Development provided the background from which Ries developed the Lean Startup approach. Lean Startup is based on the assumption that it is not possible to predict in advance how the market will react to a new product offering and in particular which features will be most liked and which will not be favoured or relevant. Thus, instead of spending a lot of money producing a finished product before offering it to the market, market feedback should be sought during the development process. This should help to avoid spending money on features that are not liked and to focus attention instead on those aspects of the project that appear to be crucial to its acceptance.

The approach arose from Ries's experience of high-tech start-ups, some of which failed despite apparently having 'a great product, a brilliant team, amazing technology and the right idea at the right time'.[3] With Blank as a mentor he looked to other industries for product development ideas and experimented with iterative product releases – limited releases of what were effectively prototypes at different development stages – so that genuine market responses could be assessed early on. This both improved the effectiveness of the development process and reduced its cost.

Those wanting to study Lean Startup further can do so through Ries's book *The Lean Startup*,

> through Blank's teachings and on line through Udacity (www.udacity.com). The main point for this book, however, is that Lean Startup acknowledges the limitations of hypothetical market research and instead seeks genuine market feedback from real product offerings, albeit at prototype stages and on a limited scale. In other words it advocates testing the market for real.

## THE EXPLORING APPROACH

Businesses tend to think in terms of market research, but explorers want to get out there and try it – possibly because they know there is no other way. In business, market research seems to be standard practice. It is what is expected and often done – although there is some evidence that its main use is not to predict market reaction but as insurance against blame if a new venture doesn't work out. Philip Graves quotes Tim Dewey, who has held senior marketing positions in several blue chip companies, as saying:

> People use different stages of research so that if the initiative is unsuccessful they can say, 'Look how thorough I was. I did my due diligence.' In my experience it comes down to the organisational culture; where there's a fear of failure research is used to avoid getting the blame for a project that fails.[4]

Explorers may do some prior research, and in the absence of a map they may try to learn as much as they can about their target from others who have been near it. But if an area is truly unexplored they know that the only way to find out what is there is to go and have a look. By all means look at what others have done, but if no one has been there before the only way to find out is to go there and have a look yourself. And, Saras Sarasvathy suggests, don't bother trying too hard to identify possible competitors and building a 'sustainable competitive advantage' until you have done some exploration and have a better idea of what opportunities there might be.[5]

Illustration 12.3   Exploring the market – for real

> For a lot of entrepreneurs starting out, the most important aspect of any new venture is exploring the viability and fit within the market. This can be done in many ways, from sitting at your desk carrying out market research, to getting out to speak to people within the industry, to carrying out some consultancy with a company within the market to identify the key market drivers and influencers. However, no matter what avenue an entrepreneur takes, the key underlying requirement is to get out there and get started. Lots of great ideas never make it past the planning stage, because all they do is plan: plan for issues that might not be present, plan for customers they don't know and plan to utilise resources they might never need.
>
> When we started [the business] we decided before cutting code we were going to talk to everyone and anyone who could add value. The key here being

## Principle 5 – The Only Reliable Test Is a Real One    117

'adding value'. The biggest mistake an entrepreneur can make is to start building something they think the market needs without figuring out does the market ACTUALLY need it. We travelled all over, from New York to LA, San Francisco to Seattle, and built a pretty clear picture on the market dynamics, what the real thorny issues were, the ones no one really wants to admit to in the industry press. With all this data we sat down and set about figuring out how to build a product that would solve a lot of issues facing games developers, brands and gamers, namely, delivering real revenue to games developers, giving brands a clear and scalable channel to connect with gamers while giving gamers something tangible to compete for, making their gaming experience both enjoyable and rewarding.

As we now had an idea of what the market wanted and saw a clear vision of how it fitted with the original aims of the founders, building a company in the gaming market that helped connect gamers to brands through games. ...

To tie all this up, the most important thing driving [the business] is our desire to test and re-test every assumption before we do anything. It might appear that there isn't a lot of planning mentioned here and to a certain extent that's true: we run on an agile development process, with product development roadmaps of no more than 3/6 months broken into 2 week sprints, allowing us to make (sic) fast and smart. We worked off a one-page business plan canvas (note no traditional business plan) that we iterated on continually, using it as a living, breathing document that kept everything contained and focussed. However, nothing will be a substitute for getting out and testing your assumption in a live market.

*Source*: Private communication from a software start-up.

### Summary of the Key Points of Chapter 12

- A number of experts are now pointing out that market research techniques are an unreliable way of trying to predict the market's response to a new venture.

- The only reliable way to see how people will actually respond to something is to do it for real by offering a real product (or service) in a real situation.

- Despite this, many businesses tend to think in terms of market research – although some are learning to do things differently. Testing for real is the assumption behind approaches such as Lean Startup. It is also what explorers do: they go and look for real instead of trying to predict from a distance what they will find.

# 13
# Principle 6 – Get Started and Get Some Momentum

> The Essence of This Chapter
>
> - It is important to get started. Too much hesitation can kill a venture.
>
> - Getting started helps to generate momentum and a sense of having done something, which provides encouragement and more incentive to keep going.

Illustration 13.1   Early perseverance can pay off

If you are hesitant about starting your new venture you can probably always find a good reason for postponing it – but that way you won't actually make any progress. Putting off something about which they are apprehensive is a common reaction by many people. It is a bit like going for a swim in cold water – once you are in it seems great but the expected shock of making the first move into the water can be an obstacle (see Illustration 13.4). So the principle is, once you have done the sensible prior checks, don't hesitate but get into it. Once you have achieved even a small amount it can provide a sense of achievement and the encouragement that comes from that. Once you have started your venture the momentum you gain will help you to surmount difficulties. If you haven't started, difficulties will only add further delay to your start.

Illustration 13.2   Ready–fire–aim

> The method adopted by competitors at shooting competitions could be described as 'ready–aim–aim–aim'[1] because they spend so much time continually checking to confirm the aim. That is because they know that, once the trigger is pulled, they will have no further control over the bullet. Therefore the aim has to be spot on, with an accurate allowance made for any contingencies such as a cross wind. If they were shooting at something in real life, often the target would be moving, which would make it even harder to get the aim right.
> In contrast, with a guided missile the approach might be described as 'ready–fire–aim'. In other words the process is to check that the missile is ready and pointed in roughly the right direction, then to get it started by firing it, and finally to

> control it onto the target. With a guided missile it is much easier to hit an erratically moving target – which is why such missiles were developed.
>
> It is important to remember that ventures can be steered, which is recognised in the 'pilot-in-the-plane' principle of effectuation. Therefore it is not necessary to spend a lot of time refining the preparation – as in the 'ready–aim–aim–aim' process, which might be typified by the business plan approach. Instead, for many new ventures, a 'ready–fire aim' attitude will be much more suitable.

There are those who argue that a lot of preparation and planning is an essential prerequisite before making any active commitment. As a respected professor of management, Henry Mintzberg might have been expected to extol formal planning, but instead he criticises it. According to him the concept of so-called 'strategic planning' originated in the mid-1960s but, he claims, it has been undermined by what he believes to be 'fundamental fallacies'.[2] Two of these fallacies are the fallacy of predetermination and the fallacy of formalisation. Under 'predetermination' he points out that successful planning requires the world to hold still, or at least unfold as predicted, while the plan is implemented – and that does not happen. Under 'formalisation' he points out that it is not possible to formalise and institutionalise things like innovation and entrepreneurship. The third fallacy he identifies is the fallacy of detachment. Organisations were supposed to have heads which think and bodies which act – because the managers in the head should be detached from, rather than being immersed in, the details of the task so that they were able to look beyond it and think strategically. To be sure, says Mintzberg, we think in order to act, but 'we also **act in order to think**' (emphasis added). We experiment and try things and, when we find that something works, we start to build our thinking around it, and doing it then becomes our strategy. That process of acting in order to think and plan, he suggests, is not some aberrant behaviour but 'the very essence of the process of strategic learning'.[3]

Illustration 13.3  The relevance of getting started and gaining momentum

> One of the authors was invited to help a group of people who were attempting to deliver a series of initiatives to improve the town in which they lived. This was some time after the group had started and it was apparent that by then they were at a stage where they needed some structure and coordination if their various initiatives were to be effective. However, the author concluded, they were probably right to have started without a plan in the way that they did – both because they had made progress and were gaining local support, which was encouraging them to persevere and because, until they had started and found opportunities, they didn't know which initiatives they would be pursuing and couldn't therefore determine what plans and models were appropriate.

A military maxim is that 'time spent on reconnaissance is seldom wasted', but Mintzberg suggests, instead, that experimentation is necessary in order to plan. Thus for an exploratory small venture it is necessary to start and to act in order to think. Provided basic checks have been made, so that a start is not likely to be foolhardy (see Chapter 11), getting started can have many benefits.

Illustration 13.4   When to reconnoitre and when to jump in?

> When going to swim, sticking your toe in the water before jumping in may be a sensible precaution if the water is likely to be too hot. But more often the water is likely to be cold and then the toe-dipping will only confirm what you already know. Of course there could be unforeseen hazards under the water, so it might be sensible to look for them first, but just sticking your toe in won't do that. In confirming the coldness of the water, it may weaken your resolve to get in and get the unpleasant initial shock over with. If you really want to swim, after a quick check, just leaping in may be psychologically easier.

An important benefit is that getting started and being active can provide a sense of progress – and thus of encouragement. Too much prior analysis can serve to delay action and induce 'analysis paralysis', because the more analysis that is conducted the greater the likelihood that you will think of other things that could be checked before starting. When taking an exam, after reading through the questions it can be very helpful to tackle an easy question first to gain an early sense of achievement and progress. Staring at a clean sheet of paper or clear computer screen can introduce writer's block, when it becomes increasingly hard to make the first move. In a similar way, having a sense of making some progress can be very helpful for any venture. In any form of movement, if you have some momentum then any difficulties encountered are less likely to stop you – whereas if you haven't yet started any difficulties will only further delay that start. Therefore it can be helpful to engineer an early sense of achievement by getting started.

That feeling of process and achievement already made will help you to keep going. Economists may tell you that the investment you have already put into a venture is a sunk cost and shouldn't influence any decisions on further investment – but instinct isn't necessarily that logical. If you really want to succeed then you may be helped by a feeling that what you have done so far obliges you to go on, and thus provides more incentive to keep going. It has been said of rock-climbing that the best way to tackle the harder climbs (assuming you do have rock-climbing skills) is not to stand back and look at the rock first but to get started. Looking at the whole of the rock can be discouraging because all the difficulties become apparent at the same time, whereas once you have started you have to keep going and address any difficulties one by one as and when they occur (see Illustration 13.5).

Illustration 13.5    The rock climbers' approach?

> Some time ago one of the authors read an article about rock-climbing, a sport which was normally of little interest. What held the author's attention was the description the article gave of rock-climbing practice. As all the easy climbs had been done, harder new ones were being attempted and, for them, climbers were finding that spending a lot of time looking at the rock before attempting to climb was counter-productive. It tended to present all the obstacles at the same time and make it seem very hard. Instead, those climbers who really wanted to get to the top found that a better approach was to get started – because, once started, they had to go forward and tackle the obstacles one by one as they arose.
>
> Does an analogy with rock-climbing have any implications for business?
>
> - Can starting, rather than planning, be the route to success? Starting means that you are in and have the momentum to go on.
>
> - Is it better to be the first up and running, or to be sure first that you are right?
>
> - But is it only for those who have some idea of what they are doing?

New venture exploration is a dynamic process. A bit like riding a bicycle, it can't be done statically. As anyone who has tried to control a boat knows, you can't steer it, re-orient it or react to other boats or to the weather unless you are under way. In many respects an enterprise is like a sailing boat. A sailing boat relies on the wind for its source of power and it needs to be steered carefully to use the wind. In a similar way an enterprise relies on the support and/or custom it can find, and it too needs to be steered to make best use of them. Neither a boat nor an enterprise can be steered until they have started to move, and anyone trying to direct them will not appreciate the pressures on them, and thus know when and in which direction to steer, until they are under way and have embarked on the journey. Trying to determine where to steer before starting doesn't work.

An aspect of knowing where to steer is not just appreciating the different pressures as progress is made, but also seeing the different opportunities – and many of these opportunities will only become apparent once the venture is under way. An explorer cannot be expected to decide which route to follow until he or she has got started, viewed the territory and found what routes, if any, appear to be available and attractive. Thus looking for opportunities (see Chapter 14) is only possible once you have started the venture.

Illustration 13.6   When prior reconnaissance may be a waste of time

> When exploring, if just you, or a small party, want to cross unsurveyed territory, then the best thing is just to do it. Explorers are explorers – they don't need someone else to explore for them first. However, if you want to take lots of people

> across new territory, like leading a big business, then exploring, reconnoitring and surveying and mapping first will be helpful so that you can indicate a suitable route for others to take.
>
> Advocates of formal prior planning acknowledge that exploration is necessary in order to determine which route to follow, but suggest that that should be part of the research that ought to be carried out before the main venture is launched. In this, however, the size of the venture is relevant. If you want to take a large body of people across uncharted territory then it probably will be sensible to reconnoitre first to find an acceptable route. Thus you find a route, check that it works, come back – and then lead the main group across. If, however, only you or a very small group are seeking to cross, then the act of finding a workable route will take you across, and once across you can keep going – there is no point in going back and doing it again. Thus for a large group separate prior reconnaissance may be beneficial, but for a small group it is a waste of time. The small group will do better to get started and try. If it doesn't work, it doesn't work – but finding that out by reconnaissance would have been no cheaper. If, however, it does work then progress will already have been made.

Therefore, for a small new venture, trying to plan everything in advance can be very wasteful, not least because the future is inevitably uncertain and cannot reliably be predicted (see Chapter 14). Instead it can be much better to recognise that until you get started you won't have a sense of momentum and you won't find the opportunities (see Chapter 15). Thus an important principle can be to get started and to get some momentum. The best time to plant a tree, it is said, is twenty years ago – but the second best time is now.

Illustration 13.7  An entrepreneur's view

> After 'bouncing from job to job, some less glamourous than others', John 'stumbled into telecoms sales'. Through his success in this he met an entrepeneur who was open to a new opportunity and persuaded him to invest in a new telephone company, which the entrepreneur then asked John to run.
>
> This, says John, was the start of his entrepreneurial career and, a decade later, the venture had grown into a multi-million pound business. However, by then he was bored so, driven by a midlife crisis/itch, he explored other avenues and thought he saw an opportunity in helping businesses to engage with social media. That is what he is now pursuing.
>
> John's views on starting a business are that it is 'tough, stressful, expensive and not for the faint hearted' – but he wanted to do something that hadn't been done before. He is not sure about the wisdom of not committing more than you can afford to lose, but does agree with the need to get started:
>
>> I think these two points sort of contradict each other. If you have fear of losing

money, then don't do it because no matter how much you budget, you are wrong. It will always be more expensive with more curve balls than you can possibly imagine. So if you start with always thinking of your 'safety net' you will fail. It's a self-fulfilling prophecy.

So on point number two a more blunt way of saying it is 'just f***ing do it'. Don't procrastinate. Don't sit in an office and sort your legals and surf the net. Do create a sales presentation, print a business card and order form and go out see if you can sell the product or service you are about to risk everything to build. Sell loads, sell way beyond those friends and family that will give you mercy sales and tell you it's a brilliant idea, beyond those so sympathetic to your cause that they inflate your ego with flattery as they say, 'I can't believe no one has done that already'!

*Source*: Private communication from a telecom entrepreneur.

## Summary of the Key Points of Chapter 13

- Too much hesitation can kill a venture. After appropriate pre-checks it is important to get started.

- Getting started helps the venture because:
  - Getting started is necessary to make progress.
  - Making progress helps to generate a sense of achievement and the encouragement that comes from that.
  - Making progress also generates momentum, which can carry the venture over obstacles.
  - It is often necessary to start exploring in order to be able to plan, rather than the other way around.
- Therefore there is a lot to be gained by making a start as early as practical.

# 14
# Principle 7 – Accept Uncertainty

> The Essence of This Chapter
> - If you can't remove uncertainty, accept it, and proceed accordingly.
> - Look for, and be ready to respond to, the unforeseen – whether obstacle or opportunity.

As an official government guide puts it: 'however well risks are identified and analysed the future is inherently uncertain'.[1] The wise new venture explorer therefore accepts this uncertainty and acts accordingly. So, because the future is largely unpredictable, control what you can control and keep a lookout for the unforeseen, which you can't control – but which might provide unexpected opportunities or obstacles. So proceed with caution – being flexible and able and prepared to react to the unexpected and to alter course should unforeseen opportunities or obstacles arise.

Uncertainty is common in nature and many organisms have evolved effective ways of proceeding in uncertain situations. As Iain McGilchrist observes:

> Watch an animal explore its environment. It tries something and then recoils, it tries something else and recoils again, but then goes

forward and onward until it recoils again – and so it finds the right path to what it is seeking. This is an intelligent way to succeed and to survive. An animal that ploughs on regardless of evidence that it is in danger will not survive.[2]

According to Henry Mintzberg, in the analysis quoted in Chapter 13, planning tends to promote strategies using predictions for the future that are based on extrapolations from the past. Unfortunately history shows us that events rarely continue for long as neat extrapolations, but sooner or later are subject to discontinuities, which will not be forecast by analytic procedures, no matter how carefully constructed.[3] Thus, instead of trying to remove the uncertainty by elaborate forecasting, it is better instead to be prepared to react quickly once a discontinuity occurs.

Risk and uncertainty are inherent in enterprise and entrepreneurship – as is recognised in Chapter 9. Richard Cantillon, who first introduced the term 'entrepreneur' into the language of economics, suggested that the three classes of actors in an economy were the landlords, who owned and rented out the land, the entrepreneurs, who often rented the land for their activities, and the hired employees, who worked for landlords or entrepreneurs. What distinguished the entrepreneurs from landlords or waged employees was that, whereas the rents or wages due to the landlords and employees respectively could be fixed in advance, the returns from the entrepreneurial activity (which for Cantillon included farming) were uncertain because they depended on many factors beyond the entrepreneurs' control. Thus inevitably the entrepreneurs operated at a risk.

## DISTINGUISHING BETWEEN RISK AND UNCERTAINTY

Today a distinction is sometimes made between risk and uncertainty, with the difference being that for risk the odds are known, or can be determined, whereas for uncertainty the odds are not known and cannot easily/realistically be determined. Or, as Donald Rumsfeld – the former US Defense Secretary, once put it:

> There are known knowns; there are things we know that we know. There are known unknowns; that is to say, there are things that we now know we don't know. But there are also unknown unknowns; there are things we do not know we don't know.[4]

The known unknowns might therefore be converted into risk because, as we know about them, we can try to assess them. Those known unknowns which cannot be easily assessed, along with the unknown unknowns (of which there are many which can face a new business) belong in the realms of uncertainty. If that distinction is used then, it would seem that much enterprise is uncertain rather than risky, especially new enterprise – and that uncertainty does not necessarily mean that the risk is considerable. The risks involved may actually be quite low, but they can't be assessed in advance. Hence the advisability of proceeding to explore them – but proceeding appropriately for an uncertain situation (and see Table 14.1).

## THE FUTURE IS UNCERTAIN

The future is uncertain and risk and uncertainty are inherent in enterprise, especially in new venture

Table 14.1 *Different operating approaches for prediction, risk and uncertainty*

| | Prediction | Risk | Uncertainty |
|---|---|---|---|
| *Assumption:* | A specific prediction can be made of what will happen | The chances of specific things happening can be estimated reasonably well | The future cannot be predicted with any degree of reliability |
| *The basis for the approach:* | Basing the prediction either on past trends or on what people say they will do in the future | Assessments of variance and possibilities based on past histories | Accepting that the future is uncertain but some factors may be influenced or controlled |
| *Selecting the route to follow:* | Refine prior efforts and strive for a perfect forecast | Prepare robust scenarios and select the one which offers the best balance of risk and reward | Proceed warily based on expertise and seeking to influence and/or control |
| *Reacting to surprises:* | Check the predictions (on the assumption that a mistake must have been made) | Assume that any surprise is a rare upset and is unlikely to happen again – so try to stick to the plan | Accept surprises and rethink the approach to take advantage of any new opportunities revealed |
| *Assessment of success:* | The extent to which the plan is implemented | The extent to which the plan is implemented | The extent to which the overall aim, or an acceptable alternative, is achieved |

*Source:* Based on S. Read, S. Sarasvathy, N. Dew, R. Wiltbank and A.-V. Ohlsson, *Effectual Entrepreneurship* (London: Routledge, 2011) p. 27.

## Principle 7 – Accept Uncertainty

exploration. The use of forecasting techniques such as those employed by market researchers may have appeared to suggest that, if enough careful research is done, the future can be predicted and uncertainty removed – but that is a false hope. As Philip Graves shows in his book *Consumer.ology* (see Illustration 3.3) 'market research cannot work' and extrapolating from historic trends cannot indicate the future discontinuities which history shows are inevitable.

The future is uncertain – so proceed accordingly. Starting a new venture is an uncertain process, but so also is living. In life we know that accidents and surprises happen, that the unexpected is actually quite common and that despite much care and preparation future events are unpredictable. How often is the favourite beaten in a sporting event or a new toy a surprising Christmas favourite? So we learn to live with uncertainty and to proceed accordingly.

Illustration 14.1   Why there can't be route maps for new ventures

> An example of trying to reduce future uncertainty is in planning journeys. If you want to drive to somewhere distant then you probably look at a road atlas and select a likely route. You might also consult others who have done the same journey and/or consult web sites. Nearer the time you might check the traffic conditions and the weather reports. All that should enable you to decide how to travel, what the journey is going to be like and how long it is likely to take. And

these days when you are actually driving you may well rely on a satnav device to direct your movements, and there are signposts to guide you.

Thus you have planned your journey and minimised the unexpected – and as a result you expect to travel relatively smoothly to your destination with few, if any, surprises. Nevertheless, the unforeseen can still happen and there can still be holdups – such as a traffic accident blocking the motorway, causing delays and/or necessitating detours away from the planned route.

But how would you do all this planning and make the journey if details of the terrain weren't yet stored in the satnav's memory, if there were no signposts and no maps existed – because maps, signposts and satnav instructions are only available if someone has already been through the territory and surveyed it? Thus it is nonsense for business plans to be described, as some do, as route maps for new ventures to follow. You can't have a map of unexplored and uncertain territory that no one has explored before. Instead new venturers are the explorers and they should operate accordingly.

## ENTREPRENEURS AND RISK

It is a myth that entrepreneurs are necessarily risk-takers – that they are born with a tolerance of uncertainty or a trait or predisposition to take risks. Nor do entrepreneurs succeed because they are better than others at forecasting the future. Instead they succeed because they operate in an appropriate way when the future is uncertain.

Enterprising people may not perceive a course of action as risky because they fully understand the situation and therefore, for them, it is not very uncertain. However, a perception of low risk can also arise because of cognitive biases: it is argued that sometimes entrepreneurs may not perceive a risk in a risky situation because they are overconfident, because they have the illusion that they are in control of a situation and because they tend to associate with optimistic people who do not dwell on failures.[5]

Stuart Read *et al.* contrast the different approach to risk shown by entrepreneurs and bankers.[6] Bankers, they suggest, used to be thought of very risk averse, but the events of the 2008 financial crisis showed that this was not the case, and many of them took very large risks. Read *et al.* point out that the difference between them and entrepreneurs lies in what they think they can control. In a given situation they found that bankers tended to look for a specific rate of return and then see how they could reduce the risk involved in achieving it. Entrepreneurs instead opted for a level of risk with which they were comfortable, which might be quite low, and then tried to increase the return they could get without exceeding that level of risk. This would explain the risks some bankers had taken before the financial collapse. If they saw others apparently making high rates of return they also targeted similar rates of return and accepted the risks involved.

Thus the entrepreneurs might be said to have accepted that the gap between what you think will happen and what actually happens is often large, and therefore limited their investment to what they could afford to lose if things didn't go as they might have expected (see Principle 2). In contrast, the bankers trusted that things would happen as they expected, because that was what had happened in the recent past, and therefore bet more than they, or their banks, could afford to lose to get the return they wanted.

## OPERATING WITH UNCERTAINTY

How should someone operate in conditions of uncertainty? Essentially, it could be said, by applying common sense. If you are able to see and are walking across a space, such as a room, which is well lit you will be able to cross confidently and quickly because you can see when the obstacles are. If, however, you are blindfolded, you will walk across the same space more hesitantly, so that, if you do encounter an unforeseen obstacle, you can stop in time before you fall over it or otherwise injure yourself.

Proceeding in the dark in that way is the essence of operating in uncertainty. You do proceed, but you realise that the unexpected can occur and you do not commit yourself so fully to a particular course that you cannot change if an unforeseen problem does arise. One of Saras Sarasvathy's principles of effectuation (see Illustration 4.4) is the *pilot-in-the-plane* principle[7] which recognises that unexpected issues will arise. A successful entrepreneur will realise that he or she is not on a set, predetermined course, but instead should have the wherewithal to steer away from, or around, an obstacle, or towards an opportunity, if one does arise.

## SOME IMPLICATIONS

The essential point is that the future is not pre-ordained so cannot reliably be predicted – and so new ventures should not invest in predictions of what will happen. Instead, as effectuation points out, because the future isn't predetermined, it can be shaped. Therefore new ventures should proceed accordingly – trying to control what they can control, trying to influence those things they can influence, and trying to stay balanced so that they are ready to respond to the unforeseen and can react accordingly should the unexpected happen – which it will.

Most opportunities, and obstacles, won't become apparent to a venture until it has got started (as suggested in the previous section). So don't start with a single, fixed, predetermined path in mind – instead act like an explorer: look for and explore likely opportunities, and don't necessarily expect the first one you try to be the best. Keep your eyes open for those opportunities, and any obstacles, because if you don't look you won't see them – to your detriment.

It is a corollary of uncertainty that some exploration will be necessary to find the best way. Some of the ways explored may not work well and identifying them is part of the route to success. Many people like to look at a range of garments, and will even try some of them on, before selecting the ones which they want to buy, and many people will not be happy that they have made the best selection until they have tried on some others. Trying on one that doesn't suit them is part of the process of finding one that does. This is to be expected as part of a successful exploration and should not therefore perceived as a failure.

If the future is uncertain and there are risks involved in venturing into it, that applies whatever you do, and staying in your present employment is also likely to have its risks. So consider both the risks of what you might lose if the enterprise fails and the risks of what you might lose if you don't try it.

> **Summary of the Key Points of Chapter 14**
>
> - If you can't remove uncertainty, accept it and act accordingly.
>
> - Don't proceed in such a way that you can't change course if an unexpected opportunity or obstacle arises.
>
> - So look for, and be ready to respond to, the unforeseen – whether obstacle or opportunity.

# 15
# Principle 8 – Look for Opportunities

> The Essence of This Chapter
> 
> - Many useful opportunities are either created by what you do or are only revealed once you have got started and can see what is out there.
> 
> - So keep your eyes open. Look for and be open to opportunities and respond to what you find.

It has been said that 'there is a saying among prospectors: "go out looking for one thing and that's all you'll ever find"'.[1] It is therefore important to keep looking out for opportunities, opportunities either to do things better or to do better things. As Illustration 7.2 indicates, in exploration the unexpected often happens and some avenues tried turn out not to be as productive as might have been hoped. However, the sensible explorer knows that several avenues should be tried – and that some of these may not be revealed until the venture is under way. One feature of the future being uncertain is that unexpected opportunities can arise or be revealed, and the new venture explorer should look out for such contingencies: whether they are opportunities for new products or services, new customers, new markets or new partnerships. However, this principle asserts not just that there is a possibility of finding new opportunities, but that this is actually what explorers do – they actively search out new possibilities and assess them. They explore because they know that the first direction they take may not turn out to be the best – so they look for other possibilities and, if they like what they see, they use those opportunities to move forward. And in new venturing those new opportunities may even be created by the venturer's exploration efforts.

In his book *Adapt*, Tim Harford, who also wrote *The Undercover Economist*, explains why 'success always starts with failure'. Success in solving many problems, he suggests comes from trying, from observing that our initial efforts aren't working, but seeing from the experience where they might be improved, making changes and then trying again. Those who can't, or won't, observe whether their efforts are working, and can't, or won't, be open to the possibility of alternatives, are the ones condemned to fail. For instance, it was said of Philip II of Spain that 'no experience of the failure of his policy could shake his belief in its essential excellence'[2] and Harford relates how some of the major failed economic projects in Stalinist Russia were the result of combining a dictator's love of grand projects with a pathological immunity to feedback and a refusal, therefore, to accept that they might not be working and to consider alternative approaches.

Thus, for Harford, success very often comes not from doing the right thing from the very start, but from starting and then seeing where changes for the better might be possible. It is like the difference between trying to hit an erratically moving target with a rifle, which has to be aimed correctly at the start, or with a guided missile, which is launched and can then be steered onto the target.

Scott Shane suggests that a new venture starts when someone sees an opportunity. As he puts it: 'the entrepreneurial process begins with the perception of the existence of opportunities'.[3] Whereas effectual explorers know that opportunities can be made as well as found.[4] For instance the original Starbucks was apparently started because its owners were passionate about good coffee – not because they saw an opportunity for a worldwide chain of coffee shops.

Therefore the views of people like Harford and Sarasvathy suggest not only that it is possible to find good opportunities for a new venture once it has started, but that it is often the better way to do it. Opportunities are both found and made. Some may be found before a venture starts, but others will only be discovered later once the venture is under way, because they are revealed by that process – along with those that are created by what the venture explorer is doing. This is another reason for not preparing a detailed business plan before the start of a new venture – because the effort is likely to be wasted if better opportunities are found or created soon after that start.

Those new opportunities may be for new products or services, new processes or new customers and markets, but they may not appear initially to be that. Therefore the venture explorer should be open to new possibilities that might be worth exploring even if it is not clear where they could lead. And it is not just in new products and markets that there might be opportunities, but also in new associates or partners. If following Principle 2 means that a new venture explorer cannot him- or herself provide all the resources needed, finding a partner who can contribute could be an advantage – so opportunities for that might also be sought.

The previous principle, Principle 7, is about acting for uncertainty and responding to the unforeseen. It advises accepting that the situation is uncertain and that the future may be largely unpredictable – and acting accordingly. That means proceeding cautiously and flexibly and being prepared to alter course if new opportunities arise. If the market is predictable it is fixed in its ways and there isn't much you can do about it. If, on the other hand, it is unpredictable, that suggests that it is not fixed and in that case it also suggests that what you do might help to change it.

Therefore, as a new venture explorer you should proceed with your eyes open, looking for new and possibly better opportunities and being ready to respond to them. If you are determined on going one way and on progressing down and/or exploring just one route, then you won't be interested in alternatives. But if you want a positive outcome then other routes that you find may be of interest because they may be better for your purposes. Are you trying to find just one thing in your exploration: for instance looking for the source of the Nile or a westward route to Japan? Or are you open to other possibilities you may encounter – such as the riches available in America (even if, like Columbus, they are not what you thought you were looking for). And even if you are looking for just one thing, if you keep your eyes open you may find a better route to it than the one you first thought of. Being open to the possibility of a better route or destination, and being ready to take advantage of it when you find it, may be the way to turn something that might otherwise be a failure into a success.

### Summary of the Key Points of Chapter 15

- Many useful opportunities will only be revealed once you have got started, or even be created by your efforts.

- Therefore, as an explorer, you should be looking actively for the best way to achieve your goal and assessing the possibilities revealed by your progress.

- Part of the process of finding the best, or at least the acceptable, may be finding and identifying those that are not acceptable.

- So keep your eyes open. Look for and be open to opportunities and respond to what you find.

# 16
# Principle 9 – Build and Use Social Capital

> The Essence of This Chapter
>
> - Social capital comes from human contacts and is a vital factor when working in a human environment.
>
> - Social capital is thus one of the capitals essential for enterprise.
>
> - Therefore it will be crucial for a new venture explorer to understand the main forms of social capital and how to build and use them.

Social capital is probably as important as financial capital for many ventures. It comes from social contacts and it is like financial capital in that it is possible to use only as much as has been acquired. It is also like vitamins in food, in that there are different varieties of it, each of which has a different use. It is therefore relevant to appreciate these different forms and understand how to acquire them.

## WHAT IS SOCIAL CAPITAL?

'No man is an island, entire of itself. Each is a piece of the continent, a part of the main.' With these words

John Donne famously emphasised the interdependence of people, and in his book *Herd*, Mark Earls has also stressed the social nature of human existence:

> The influence of others is to be found in every aspect of our lives, in the big and the small things we do. We cannot escape it; even if we pretend we are superior and highly principled and self-determining, we all do it all of the time. We are Super Social Apes.[1]

Ventures, enterprises and businesses are made and run by people, and as both Donne and Earls indicate in their separate ways, people are socially connected and influenced. This can affect everything they do, including new venture exploration. Human connections have always been important, but that has not always been recognised in business. For instance, they have received little recognition in classical economics or been listed among the requirements for a successful enterprise. Now, however, the impact of inter-personal links is receiving more recognition, and although there does not yet seem to be a single widely accepted word for them, the term 'social capital' is gaining greater acceptance.

Although the term 'social capital' was apparently first used in 1916,[2] it is still not well understood and does not have a single clear definition. Nevertheless, it is suggested here that the term is helpful because the word 'social' highlights the social nature of the connections in question and the word 'capital' suggests that, like financial capital, it is something that needs to be acquired before it can be used, and is not inexhaustible. It also suggests that its importance for any enterprise should be recognised – which is why understanding and using social capital is a key principle for all new venture explorers.

## USING SOCIAL CAPITAL

Despite its usefulness there are few guides to how to build and use social capital. And despite its relevance to enterprise it does not feature in traditional business plan formats, or in the sort of enterprise training that is based on them. So, unlike the preparation of those business plans, there are no standard formulae available for the acquisition and use of social capital. This book therefore suggests the following pointers.

### The Different Forms of Social Capital That Might Be Helpful

So far there is no definitive list of the different forms of social capital. However, any of the following might be helpful to enterprise and new venture explorers:

- *A supportive environment.* It has often been ignored within listings of helpful inputs to enterprise, but a supportive social environment that regards enterprise as an acceptable, and even desirable, form of work, is often the first requirement. (See Illustration 16.1.)

- *Guidance.* Without a suitably supportive environment some people may never try venturing for themselves, and therefore never need other forms of social capital helpful for venture exploration. But if they do try it then the first help they may need from their contacts is guidance in aspects of how to go about it.

- *Information.* Another need is likely to be information about many aspects of venturing, such as legal and regulatory requirements, market information, and what support might be available. Some of this can be found from published sources, from the Internet and from enterprise agencies – but personal sources may often be helpful, if only to interpret information.

- *How to do things and how things are done.* In any new venture the official rules are likely to be an incomplete, and often obtuse, guide to how to do things. Advice from someone involved and with relevant practical experience can be very useful.

- *Connections and contacts for advice, custom, supply, partnerships etc.* Official sources are also unlikely to be able to make helpful introductions. A venture is likely to require suppliers, customers and professional advisers such as accountants. It may also benefit from doing things in partnership, formally or informally, with others – so introductions to all or any of these can help.

- *Advocacy, references and referrals.* In many areas of work, references can help. So people who know and are prepared to vouch for the excellence of your work can be very useful – and people who will help to present your offer to others and who like you and/or your venture so much that they refer people to you.

Illustration 16.1  A social capital example: The importance of a supportive social circle

> A business mentor told one of the authors about a young man she was trying to help. After having been unemployed for a period he was trying to establish himself as a contract gardener but was getting nuisance calls to his business phone number late at night. Knowing his circumstances, the mentor suspected that they might be from his former mates, most of whom were still unemployed, and who might resent his deviation from that norm. If that was correct, the calls were, in effect, negative social capital which was discouraging the young man. So the mentor suggested that he should try to change his friends and associate instead with people who might be more encouraging. It is thus important for new venture explorers to appreciate that having positive friends can be a helpful form of social capital.
>
> This example is a small demonstration that society's unwritten, and unofficial, 'rules' can be very influential. As Baumol has suggested in his historical analysis of entrepreneurship (see Illustration 23.2), if an activity such as productive entrepreneurship is not very socially acceptable, then few people will engage in it. Behaviour is catching – it has been said that obesity is contagious like a virus, which you catch by mixing with obese people[3] and that, if you want to be happy, choose happy friends. So mix with people who are likely to encourage you in your endeavour. Trying to grow enterprise in an

> anti-enterprise culture is like trying to give up smoking when surrounded by smokers or to grow alkaline-liking plants in acid soil. So if you find yourself in the wrong sort of environment, try to create a better one by choosing to mix with different friends who will support and encourage you in your endeavour.
>
> A supportive social environment often consists of some or all of the five Ps: partners (personal and business), pals, peers, parents and other influential people. Such groups, which can be big or small, can be influential. The examples of young people taking up smoking to emulate their peers or joining gangs to feel included show how pervasive a social influence can be. So your supportive social environment doesn't have to be a big group – just enough to let you feel that those whose opinion you value in turn value what you are doing.

**The Different Sorts of People Who Might Be Helpful**

It is also to be expected that different forms of social capital will often come from different people, including:

- *Advocates and referees*. People who can vouch for you and/or provide references and referrals.

- *Mentors*. People who might act as mentors (and see under 'Mentors' in Further Information).

- *Connectors*. People who know, and can therefore introduce you to, customers, suppliers and/or potential partners.

- *Sources of information.* People with relevant information, for instance about sources of support or the norms of a particular industry.

- *Role models.* People who provide you with an example to emulate and who show you what can be done.

- *Team substitutes.* A wider team in a bigger venture can provide a useful mix of complementary skills such as someone who can see the bigger picture and someone who can focus on the detail, someone who keeps things going and someone who can focus on meeting deadlines. So anyone trying a venture on their own, or with just one or two partners, can lack some of those inputs. Such a venture may need to look elsewhere for contributors, such as:

    – Someone to push them and/or make them think.

    – Someone to offer encouragement and praise.

    – Someone to be a devil's advocate and criticise when necessary.

Illustration 16.2    Finding a mentor

- A simple formula for how to get started in business is indicated in *The Beermat Entrepreneur*.[4] It lists just three things that you need: your elevator pitch, a mentor and your first customer.

- The purpose of mentoring has been stated as being 'to support and encourage people to manage their own learning ... in order to become the person they want to be'.[5] Having a mentor may be the application of a particular component of social capital, but it can nevertheless be a crucial one.

- There are organisations, such as the Prince's Trust, which try to allocate mentors to the people they help, and which therefore assemble lists of potential mentors upon whom they can call. However, in such cases you are allocated a mentor – you don't choose one – and choosing one yourself can be much more effective because then you are much more likely both to get a suitable mentor and to be actively involved in the mentoring process, rather than just being a passive recipient of mentoring advice.

- How can you choose a mentor? There is a guide to this process also in *The Beermat Entrepreneur*, which has some useful tips. The core of it, however, amounts to identifying someone with the knowledge, experience and/or contacts that you think could be useful and then asking them. That appears to be what many of the competitors in the television show *Dragons' Den* are doing: they are looking for a suitable mentor (or mentors) with good social capital, with the financial contribution the programme insists on actually being a secondary consideration.

Table 16.1 *Some of the benefits available from networks*

- *Information.* Entrepreneurs use their social networks to signal their intentions and to gather information about potential opportunities.

- *Sponsorship and support.* Family and friends will not only provide introductions into appropriate networks, but will also offer emotional and tangible support.

- *Credibility.* Membership of the network gives added weight to the evaluation of skills. Family and friends can provide credibility in areas unfamiliar to the entrepreneur.

- *Control.* Membership of the network, and assistance from it, require certain standards of behaviour. Owner-managers who do not conduct their business in a way that is acceptable to the community will quickly find themselves, and their businesses, isolated.

- *Business.* There are market networks of customers, suppliers and partners as well as production networks of sub-contractors, consultants and service suppliers. In addition, there are networks of firms that may work together on projects on a basis of collaboration. This structure can provide all the components necessary for a project without the need for 'vertical integration'.

- *Resources.* Friends and family can also be sources of resource for a new small business, and many businesses are assisted by the informal venture capital market that their owners access through their networks.

*Source*: Based in part on M. S. Greico, 'Social networks in labour migration', in *Industrial Relations Journal*, December 1985 quoted in S. Birley and S. Cromie, 'Social networks and entrepreneurship in Northern Ireland', paper presented at the *Enterprise in Action Conference*, Belfast, September 1998.

## Table 16.2 Some 'rules of the road' for networking

- Accept that entrepreneurial know-who is as important as entrepreneurial know-how.
- Be systematic, explicit and proactive in managing your network.
- Identify the central core of your own personal distinctive entrepreneurial competence.
- Your personal network is unique.
- Personal networks of entrepreneurs should include different actors and types of linkages depending on the type of ventures being pursued.
- Locate your business venture geographically as close as possible to existing support services provided by the personal networks of successful entrepreneurs.
- Be alert to different cultural and contextual norms of other actors.
- Remember that reciprocity is a universal cultural norm.
- Use your network. The strengths and weaknesses of your personal network become apparent only when it is used.
- Identify and communicate continuously with the gatekeepers in your network.
- Contact more than one individual in your network to check qualitative data and opinions.
- Be careful not to divulge confidential information that may harm you or your network members.
- Be cognizant of the relative power relationships within your network.
- Look at the contacts within your network as linkages that are negotiated using a win–win strategy.
- Assess your personal network periodically in terms of the entrepreneurial support it is supposed to give.
- Finally, don't spend too much time on managing your network.

*Source*: Based on R. Peterson and R. Rondstadt, 'A Silent Strength: Entrepreneurial Know Who', *IMD report on the 16th European Small Business Seminar Sweden September 1986*, Brussels: EFMD 86/4.

## How and Where to Find Social Capital

It is suggested above that the label 'social capital' is useful because the word 'social' indicates that it is concerned with social connections and the word 'capital' suggests that it is like financial capital, which has to be accumulated to be used. Also, like financial capital, social capital is usually the result of a two-way exchange and can be lost as well as gained. It can be acquired deliberately, but it has to be earned and accumulated if it is to be available for use. It should therefore be used wisely, as it can be exhausted.

However, with so many possible sorts of social capital and so many different possible sources, there is no single simple system for finding them. The following are five key principles to follow and Tables 16.1 and 16.2 offer some other ideas and tips:

- Understand what social capital is.
- Understand the nature of its acquisition and use.
- Look for opportunities to acquire it.
- Build a stock of it.
- Practice using it.

## CONCLUSIONS

Social capital comes from social contacts, and anyone wanting to start an enterprise should build, and use, social capital. Some indications of the various forms of social capital that might be helpful, and how they might be acquired, are given above. However, as explained at the beginning of the chapter, the study of social capital is relatively young, so there are many ideas about it and no single accepted view.

Although it may not yet be fully understood, social capital is nevertheless essential for an enterprise. Just as vitamins are crucial for health, as well as other components of food, such as protein, so social capital is necessary for enterprise, as well as other inputs, such as financial capital. Social capital is like financial capital in that you can only use as much as you have acquired, but it is also like vitamins in that there are different varieties of it, each of which has a different use.

Therefore a new venture explorer should be aware of what sorts of social capital will help and how to acquire and use them.

---

Summary of the Key Points of Chapter 16

- Social capital is one of the capitals essential for enterprise and can be as important as financial capital for new ventures.

- Social capital comes from human contacts and is a vital factor when working in a human environment.

- There are different forms and uses of social capital. So new venture explorers should understand the main forms of social capital and learn how to build and use them to their advantage.

# 17
# Principle 10 – Acquire the Relevant Skills

> **The Essence of This Chapter**
>
> - Some skills and knowledge will be essential for the successful delivery of a venture. In particular, financial management, marketing and sales, and the appropriate production ability are generally necessary for any venture.
>
> - Therefore, if you don't already have the relevant skills and/or knowledge, cultivate them or find someone with them who can help you.

Whatever your enterprise is, it is likely that you will need some skills if you are to realise it successfully. Just as an animal needs food to sustain its life and to enable it to grow, so an enterprise needs resources, or the money with which to buy them, if it is to survive to achieve its purpose (see Principle 1). Those resources, or that money, are generally obtained by trading with others by supplying something they want in exchange. Even a charity soliciting donations is providing its donors with a clean conscience and/or a sense of having made a beneficial contribution.

Thus, to run an enterprise, you will need to able to undertake those activities. That is what is indicated in Illustration 17.1, albeit in a business context.

It identifies three areas of activity in which some competence is a prerequisite. These are applicable to any enterprise and could be stated as the ability to undertake the work of the enterprise (for instance producing the goods or services it supplies), the ability to generate resources for that activity (for instance by selling the goods or service to others), and the ability to manage the resources upon which the enterprise is dependent (for instance looking after the money it generates and spends). If the enterprise has employees a fourth activity might be added to this list of generally necessary abilities, which is that of managing the people who work for the enterprise.

Illustration 17.1    The 'Management Trinity'

'No matter how big or small a business is, three areas of activity need to be taken care of:

- the technical skills necessary to produce the goods or services one wishes to sell (whether they be shoes or package tours)

- the ability to market one's goods or services

- the ability to financially manage one's affairs.

These three areas I call the "Management Trinity". If any one of the above is missing, the business is not a business, it shouldn't be called one, and it will never succeed'.

Source: Ernesto Sirolli, *Ripples from the Zambezi* (Canada, Gabriola Island: New Society Publishers, 2005), p. 92.

It is possible to add to this list – and the skills and associated knowledge of overall leadership are one possibility, as well as other skills required for specific enterprises. The following might therefore be a fuller starting list:

- The ability to produce the output in question.

- The ability to generate resources (marketing and selling) by tuning the output to what the market needs and persuading people to 'buy' it.

- The ability to manage the money and/or resources involved.

- The ability to manage the people involved.

- The ability to organise the process.

- And the ability to stand back and view the enterprise objectively.

The point is that there are likely to be areas of skill and/or knowledge that you are going to need. So it is worth considering how you might access them:

- Do you have any of them already? If so, do you know enough or would it be advisable to refine your knowledge? Would a refresher or an update be helpful?

- Can you fill in any gaps by learning new skills?

- Do you have, or can you find, partners or associates with a complementary blend of expertise?

- Can you find an adviser (paid or unpaid) or mentor who could guide you in those areas in which your own expertise is weak? This can be an important function of social capital (see Principle 9).

- Can you hire employees with the skills you lack?

**Illustration 17.2   Can you do it all yourself?**

> Ernesto Sirolli (who is the source of the comment in Illustration 17.1) is on record as saying that he doesn't think any one person can perform well in all the three areas of activity covered by the 'management trinity'. However, many people have successfully run one-person businesses, including the authors of this book, without thinking that they lacked some of the necessary ability. In most cases, while you do need some ability in the main areas indicated, you can run a thriving venture without necessarily having a lot of ability in all the areas.
>
> But if you don't have enough of one of the relevant skills, recognising that is not always easy. You have to believe in yourself, otherwise you would not be trying a new venture, but at the same time you need to be open to the possibility that you can't do everything. Human beings do unconsciously rationalise (see Illustration 18.1) and so can easily find that there appears to be a rational reason why they don't need to learn more.
>
> So how do you notice something is missing if it has never been there – that you need something you have never had? You probably need to listen to others who can better take an overall and more objective view. For instance, you can seek feedback and find an appropriate mentor (see Illustration 16.2).

## Principle 10 – Acquire the Relevant Skills

A range of abilities is necessary for the successful running of any enterprise. Probably few people have the ability and aptitude to develop a high level of competence in all of the necessary skills. Others may have enough, even if it is not all at a high level. But the main lesson may be that most people could run a better enterprise if they were to recognise which abilities they lack and then find ways of acquiring them – which will often be either by trying to learn them and/or by finding others with those abilities who will help in some way.

---

Summary of the Key Points of Chapter 17

- There are some skills and knowledge which are likely to be essential for the successful delivery of any venture – for instance ability in financial management, in marketing and sales, in the appropriate production functions, and in managing people.

- People running an enterprise need either to possess, or have access to, all such skills.

- Many people will not be expert in all these areas, although some may have enough of them to run a reasonably successful venture. However, even they might still benefit from either improving those skills or finding other people with complementary skills who will help.

# 18
# Following the Principles

> **The Essence of This Chapter**
>
> - The principles themselves are the guidance. So providing guidance in how to use them seems somewhat tautological.
>
> - Nevertheless, this chapter provides some brief comments on their use.
>
> - The principles don't do the exploring but do help the explorer to do it for him- or herself.

At this stage some readers may be looking for the equivalent of the assembly instructions – some form of guidance in how to put the principles together to create a new venture. Unfortunately they are going to be disappointed.

The principles themselves are the guidance for new venture exploration – so providing guidance in how to best to follow the principles is like providing instructions in how to use assembly instructions. However, no doubt there are people who think that with some assembly instructions further guidance is indeed necessary – so, just in case that should be the case with these principles, here are some comments about their application, albeit short reflections.

First a comment about their sequence. Because it is not possible to present all ten principles simultaneously, they have to be described one by one. Also, the principles are not like assembly instructions which have to be followed sequentially otherwise they will not work. The principles are not sequential and they are not compulsory – although they are sensible so it may be wise to follow them. Those principles which tend to be particularly relevant before the start, or in the very early stages, of a venture are described first – but there is not much more significance to the order of their presentation than that. The principles are not step-by step instructions; they aren't meant to be followed sequentially but as and when applicable.

Another feature of the principles is that they do not address ten completely separate issues. There are links between the principles, but that should not be surprising because all of them are about exploring – so it ought to be expected that they would be interlinked. These are just some of those links:

- Not committing more than you can afford to lose is linked to the need sometimes to build partnerships for which having the right sort of social capital can be essential.

- Starting from where you are includes building on the skills and knowledge you have – and that minimises the need to acquire other relevant skills.

- Carrying out reality checks and plans before starting seems to be in opposition to the need to get started and the only reliable test being a real one. But contrasting those three principles highlights the need to strike a balance between prior checking, which might tend to *disprove* but can't *prove*, and the reality that getting on and exploring is the only definitive way to find out.

- Accepting uncertainty and proceeding accordingly is an important preparation for looking for, and then building on, unforeseen opportunities.

Also, as pointed out in Chapter 9, the principles are not inviolable laws – they can be ignored but are still sensible advice. As has been said of other advice, they are for the obedience of the foolish and the guidance of the wise.

Finally, it is important to emphasise that following the principles does not remove the need to think. The principles are offered as an aid and guide to the thinking that an explorer must do. They can point out some of the possible pitfalls, highlight some of the possible approaches, and suggest some other ways of looking at things. But they don't do the exploring for the explorer, although it is hoped that they will at least help the explorer to do it for him- or herself. If, after considering the principles, you still want something more definite, like a map to show you where to go – then maybe you are not an explorer, in which case others will most likely get there first and reap the rewards of their ventures.

Illustration 18.1   Beware of instinctive rationalisations

> As an extra warning (and because it didn't seem to fit well anywhere else), beware of instinctive rationalisations. As humans we don't always appreciate why we do things but, because we like to think that we are rational beings, we unconsciously invent reasons to justify our actions.

Philip Graves refers to this tendency when he presents reasons why many answers to market research questions are unintentionally inaccurate:

> People can post-rationalize, and ... are convinced that consciousness drives their actions, even when it doesn't and that their conscious self-analysis must be accurate. ... The problem is that ... we often don't know what really caused us to behave in the way we did, although our misguided confidence in post-rationalizing makes false accounts in research seem compelling.[1]

Or, as Benjamin Franklin put it, 'so convenient a thing it is to be a reasonable creature, since it enables one to find or make a reason for everything one had in mind to do'.[2]

Even our traditional economic analysis has not recognised this, although that may be changing. According to Pete Linn, 'it is no exaggeration to say that orthodox economics is based on the idea that people can be treated, for economic purposes, as if they are selfish, independent calculating machines. Yet behavioural economics is busy proving that, in reality, people do not behave like selfish, independent calculating machines; in many cases, we do not even come close to behaving this way'.[3]

Therefore when venturing with people, whether as partners, supporters, suppliers or customers, it can be relevant to distinguish real motives from invented ones.

### Summary of the Key Points of Chapter 18

- The principles themselves are the guidance for creating a new venture. Providing guidance in how to use them seems somewhat unnecessary.

- The principles are not sequential. Neither are they separate, but instead they are interlinked.

- The principles don't remove the need to think, but are designed to guide that thinking.

- If you still want a detailed map to show you where to go, maybe you are not an explorer. In that case others will most likely get there first and take the prizes.

# Part III
# Seeking a Balanced Perspective

> Key Learning Objectives
>
> This part presents a comparison between the business-plan-based and the exploration-based approaches. From it the reader should learn that:
>
> - Sometimes it is necessary to criticise one side of an argument in order to establish a more balanced perspective.
>
> - Some form of planning is needed for all new ventures – but it does not have to be the traditional business plan.
>
> - A comparison between the business-plan-based approach and the proposed exploration-based approach indicates that both approaches have their advantages and disadvantages.
>
> - The two approaches should be treated as two tools with different uses, neither of which will always be the best approach in every situation.
>
> - However, for many new small venture start-ups, the exploration approach will often be a better tool to use. Therefore those who seek to advise and assist such start-ups should recognise this and adjust their methods and thinking accordingly.

Planning in some form may be necessary, but this book does contend that, for many new venture explorers, the business plan is not a useful form of planning – and that it may even be harmful. It also contends that the business plan is often assumed to encompass all the key considerations for a new venture and is thus used as a guide for start-up training courses – which is also misleading.

Part I of this book explains why the business plan approach is frequently advocated for new businesses, even though often it may not be appropriate, and Part II then presents an alternative approach based on a set of principles for new venture explorers. Having thus provided the justification for considering a new approach by criticising the business plan and presenting a rationale for the suggested alternative, this part of the book can now compare and contrast the two approaches with the aim of providing a balanced and constructive view of their respective merits and identifying when it might be advantageous to use each of them. However, in indicating the arguments on each side and their implications, it does revisit or allude to some points made earlier.

Chapter 19 presents the case for a balanced perspective and Chapter 20 then compares and contrasts the business-plan-based and exploration-based approaches. Chapter 21 highlights some consequent conclusions, reflections and lessons, and finally Chapter 22 reinforces the exploration message and the relevance of the ten principles for new venture explorers.

# 19
# Striking a Balance

> The Essence of This Chapter
>
> - This book does not criticise all forms of planning. Some planning is necessary for any venture exploration.
>
> - However, the book does criticise the business plan as a suitable approach for many new ventures.
>
> - That criticism may seem harsh, but it is thought to be necessary to redress the balance because the business plan is so often advocated.
>
> - This should thus help to establish a more balanced perspective for a comparison between the business plan and exploration-based approaches.

## PREPARING FOR THE FUTURE

Part I of this book argues that the business plan is not a suitable guide for many new enterprises. This is not, however, a criticism of all forms of planning. Some forward thinking is clearly required for any venture and, in any case, planning is not a simple issue. It can take many different forms – so a criticism of one form is not necessarily a criticism of another.

In any case, planning is dependent for its effect on how it is executed. Henry Mintzberg quotes the words of a US Army officer: 'any damn fool can write a plan. It's the execution that gets you all screwed up'.[1] Mintzberg also contrasts deliberate strategy, which is supposed to be fully thought through in advance, with emergent strategy, which responds to the situation as it evolves, and with variations such as umbrella strategies which set deliberately broad outlines within which the details are then allowed to emerge.

Planning is essentially about making preparations for the future and can involve one or more of the following:

- Thinking about the future
- Predicting the future
- Controlling the future
- Making specific provision for the future
- Preparing for possible future eventualities
- Preparing to act in the future.

Thus plans can vary from thoughts about what might be the response to a number of possibilities to a detailed series of specific actions to be carried out in the expectation of a specific happening. Also, there are different methods that can be applied in predicting what might happen. Some opt for a mechanistic extrapolation from present trends and others rely more on intuition. Mintzberg, in his analysis of planning, acknowledges the role of intuition. However, he points out that processes that are not verifiably objective, of which intuition is a good example, tend to be dismissed by planners, whereas other processes that seem to be formally rational, such as planning itself, are embraced as exemplary. However, he adds that because intuition is not formally rational that does not necessarily mean that it is irrational.[2]

Thus, it is suggested, the issue should not be whether to plan or not, but the extent to which it is sensible to plan for a future which is to at least some extent uncertain. It is the same in many aspects of life. For instance, if you are invited to a wedding there are a number of preparatory steps which you might think it would be sensible to take, such as accepting the invitation, arranging to take the time off work, making childcare arrangements and thinking of a suitable wedding gift. You might even want to make an appointment to have your hair done on the morning of the wedding and to find out where the venue is and where the reception will be held. However, you might not plan your precise departure time very far in advance because it might depend on the weather and traffic conditions on the day.

So what sort of planning is relevant for a new enterprise – and is the traditional business plan appropriate? This book has been critical of the business plan, but is that a fair assessment for which a balanced perspective is needed?

## RESTORING THE BALANCE

In the *Rise and Fall of Strategic Planning*, Henry Mintzberg devotes a considerable part of the book to a critical analysis of what is wrong with planning in general and strategic planning in particular. However, he explains that, having presented a negative view, he can then try to look constructively at both sides:

> We have been highly critical throughout this discussion, concerned that by trying to be everything, planning has risked being dismissed as nothing. In fact, we never had any intention of so dismissing planning, although the tone of our discussion may well have given that impression. Instead, by overstating our criticisms, we have tried to draw the debate on planning to a more viable middle ground, away from the conclusion that planning can do either everything or nothing. To draw from one extreme (where we believe planning has always been) toward the middle, one has to pull from the far end (much as in trying to balance a seesaw with all the weight on one end, one has to put weight on the other end, not the middle). Having (we hope) succeeded in drawing the reader toward that middle, we can now position ourselves there as well to consider the viable roles that planning as well as plans and planners can play in organizations. Hence the tone of our discussion changes at this point, from critical to constructive.[3]

Thus, in order to restore some sort of equilibrium and the basis for a more balanced perspective it may be necessary to add a significant amount of criticism to one side or praise to the other. As Iain McGilchrist says, when discussing the role of the two different sides of human brains (which may have a relevance for the business plan – see Chapter 21):

> If I seem to have a lot to say in favour of the right hemisphere in the book, it is because there was a balance here that needed to be redressed – and still does. A completely false view prevailed that the right hemisphere was somehow airy-fairy and unreliable and simply added some emotional colour to the perceptions of the 'intelligent' left hemisphere. But it is in reality the right hemisphere that sees more, that is more in touch with reality, and is more intellectually sophisticated.[4]

The purpose of this book is not primarily to present a criticism of the business plan. However, the business plan has been widely advocated as if no other approach is needed or worth considering, and this book therefore makes its criticism in an effort to present the case for an alternative. In this way it seeks to create the conditions needed for a more balanced perspective and a more equitable comparison between the business plan and the alternative offered.

---

Summary of the Key Points of Chapter 19

- This book does not criticise all forms of planning. Some form of planning is necessary for any venture.

- However, Part I does criticise the business-plan-based approach, which is often advocated as essential for new enterprises. That criticism may seem harsh, but it serves to demonstrate the need for another way (or ways) and to prepare the reader for the presentation, in Part II, of the exploration-based approach.

- Thus the criticism is necessary to establish a more balanced perspective as the basis for a meaningful comparison of the alternatives.

# 20
# Comparing Approaches

---

The Essence of This Chapter

- The two main approaches considered in this book are an exploration-based approach, for which the ten principles are suggested as a guide, and the business plan approach still often advocated.

- These two approaches are described separately in Parts I and II. This chapter compares them.

- It highlights the main features in each approach and contrasts their key advantages and disadvantages.

---

## THE TWO APPROACHES

Chapter 4 acknowledges that there are a number of guides available for different types or aspects of the start-up process. However, it also indicates that these guides are generally not as widely applicable as is claimed for the business plan or proposed for the exploration alternative. It is therefore on these two approaches that this chapter is focussed – first to highlight their differences and their relevant criteria and then to indicate their advantages and disadvantages.

But to start that comparison here is a summary of their key features.

## A Business-Plan-Based Approach

Planning might be likened to firing a gun at a target. In order to hit the target it is necessary to allow for the range, the wind and any movement of the target, and then to take aim and pull the trigger – hoping that the aim is good enough. Often, when the target is moving in an unpredictable fashion, the result is a miss. With a guided missile, however, once fired it is not a matter of just sitting back and hoping because the missile can be steered onto the target wherever it moves. Similarly, with a new venture, planning can encourage an attitude of 'fire and forget', which requires very careful prior calculation but still often misses, whereas effectuation is like a guided missile which is roughly aimed, quickly fired and then steered onto the target based on commitment to the task and feedback on what is actually happening.

Another feature of the traditional business plan approach is that it involves not only making and then following a business plan that determines the preferred route for the business in advance, but also prior preparation, which is often informed and directed by the framework of the traditional business plan components. Thus it is typified by the sequence outlined in Table 2.1, p. 16.

This approach thus recognises that the future may be uncertain, but seeks to reduce that uncertainty by prior investigation and planning. In particular, for business ventures it assumes that prior market research can help to indicate what can, or cannot, be sold, in what volumes and at what price. By costing what is involved in making the sales and comparing that with the income that might be generated, the profitability of the venture can be assessed against different sales projections. Thus, it is apparently believed, the odds of success can be estimated and uncertainty changed into risk, so that a risk–benefit assessment can be made as the basis for a decision on whether to proceed. Appropriate dispositions can then be made and the venture, if started, should be directed along the route indicated in the plan.

### An Exploration Approach – Accepting Uncertainty

The alternative approach advocated by this book is referred to as an 'exploration' approach, because it considers that early-stage entrepreneurship has more in common with exploration than with running a big business. It accepts that the future is uncertain and unpredictable and therefore suggests proceeding to explore it accordingly. Thus, based in part on the principles of 'effectuation',[1] ten principles are suggested as the guidance which is the basis of this approach. It is these principles that are explained in Part II.

This approach is similar to the attitude adopted by explorers seeking a way through unmapped territory. They cannot plan their route in advance because there are too many unknowns. So when they start they look for a promising path to take them in the direction they want to go, but they are open to apparently better opportunities when they discover them and they know that they may not discover them until they get started. Nevertheless, because there is no certain way through, they know that they should not commit more than they can afford to lose to a route that has not yet been proven. Therefore they try to decide which is the most attractive path to take initially from where they are, but they remain open to others and stay flexible so that with relative ease they can go round any obstacles they encounter, and switch paths, or even goals, if that seems more attractive and/or appropriate.

However, the relevance of this alternative may be obscured to some extent because its use is not acknowledged. The authors have found that, in talking to people who have started their own business, quite a few admit that, in their case, they had not done a business plan as it didn't seem to be relevant. They included some academics who had taught business plans and yet started businesses in areas such as marketing, training and consulting without doing plans themselves. They hadn't admitted this before because they seemed to feel that they were being lazy or were just a rare exception. Despite its lack of relevance in their own cases, they still seemed to accept the business plan approach as the general rule.

## THE TWO APPROACHES COMPARED

In Saras Sarasvathy's terminology,[2] exploration in the way advocated here is an 'effectuation' approach, and a business plan approach a 'causation' approach. Sarasvathy uses a cooking analogy to explain the differences, suggesting that in cooking it would be causation if you started by selecting a specific recipe, assembled the ingredients it specifies in the indicated amounts and then, following what the recipe says, put it all together to produce (you hope) a dish like the one the recipe describes. For an effectuation approach you would instead start with what you already have, such as the ingredients in the fridge and/or the cupboard, and then use your imagination, informed by an understanding of the logic of the cooking process, to put them together to create a meal in the way that you fancy (see Chapter 10).

Of course in cooking it is possible to mix causation and effectuation by taking a pre-written recipe and adapting it to your circumstances, although some would argue that such a flexible approach is the essence of effectuation because then you will produce your dish and not the recipe's dish. Similarly it is possible, while following an exploration approach, to produce a business plan if and when one is required for a prospective funder or other potential stakeholder, but that plan should not dictate the development process of the venture.

Nevertheless the two approaches are different, and thus potentially appropriate for different stages and circumstances. One of the key differences between the approaches is the attitude taken to the future. The exploration approach is based on a belief that the future is uncertain and unpredictable, and this has a number of consequences:

- If the future is unpredictable then trying to forecast it, for instance by market research, is likely to be a waste of effort. Sarasvathy found that the 'expert entrepreneurs' (people who had taken at least one company public) distrusted market research[3] and this belief is consistent with the message of observers like Philip Graves that 'the findings obtained from most market research are completely unreliable'.[4]

- On the other hand, if the future is unpredictable, that means it is not yet determined – which in turn indicates that the entrepreneur could have an opportunity to shape it.

- Because the future is uncertain this should be allowed for in how an entrepreneur operates. He or she should be on the lookout for other opportunities and/or be prepared for obstacles, and ready to react accordingly.

This distinction between the two approaches is reflected in the different ways in which they treat uncertainty and risk. If the difference between uncertainty and risk is that uncertainty means that the odds are not known whereas risk implies that they are, then a business plan approach tries to reduce uncertainty by assessing risk through research and prediction. The heart of a business plan is generally the sales forecast based on some form of market research. It is on this forecast that the projected production capacity and staffing requirements and consequent financial projections, profitability estimates and sensitivity analysis can then be based. The consequence of doing this is that, if the market research is not reliable, the plan is based on sand. Such a dubious foundation sets limits on the venture, and indeed restricts the thinking of the new venture explorer, with no compensating advantages.

In contrast, the exploration approach accepts that the future is uncertain but, instead of apparently futile attempts to try to quantify the risk before starting, it suggests starting (but proceeding in accordance with the uncertainty) to find out what the situation actually is.

The two approaches thus encourage different mindsets. The effort that has gone into preparing a business plan encourages a sense of its worth and this, together with the apparent removal, or at least reduction, of uncertainty, combined with the way that the future of the venture has been 'mapped' out, tends to set psychological blinkers. Once the plan has been developed the focus is then on realising it and the perceived horizons are those of the plan, because the plan's projections shape the anticipated dimensions of the business and its expected potential, however limited that is. In contrast, the focus of an exploration approach is on looking for possibilities, while also minimising the associated damage should they not appear. It is not a focus on the current path, which might change, but on what the path may lead to in terms of goals, or better routes to those goals, or even new goals. Thus it is about ends, not means, and on action, not analysis. Ultimately goals will not be achieved by doing nothing, so exploration is about getting started in order to find the best route, whereas a business plan is about trying to identify and prove the route before any action is initiated.

This suggests that an exploration approach is likely to appeal to venturers – people seeking to start a new venture – and to assist them in their endeavours. A business plan approach, however, may be more likely to appeal to their advisers and supporters, because they often have different objectives. Venturers, especially if they follow the principle of not committing more than they can afford to lose, generally stand to gain more if their venture succeeds that they might lose if it fails. This is especially true once they have started, as a large portion of any investment is likely by then to be a 'sunk cost'. Also they know that in order to succeed it is necessary to get started. That is not the case, however, for many people providing venture advice, funding or support – especially those doing it on a professional basis. Unless they have a stake in any profits, such supporters have more to lose if a venture fails than they will gain if it succeeds well. That is because, once their input is made, for instance their advice given or their loan terms agreed, greater success of the venture, while welcome, will bring no extra return. Failure, on the other hand, is likely to bring a loss of their stake, such as a loan, a grant or even of their reputation, as well as possible blame for being involved in or associated with a failure – and this is symptomatic of big business thinking. Thus their prime concern will be to avoid failure rather than to achieve success – and not getting started is one way of avoiding failure.

Advisers and supporters are therefore likely to be cautious and, in the extreme, they might prefer it if ventures didn't start rather than that there should be any reasonable possibility of failure if they do start (and see under 'Caution' in Further Information). Business plans suit them because they involve checks and assessments, and are based on the apparent reassurance of market research. For those starting a venture, however, maximising the chance of success is more important than minimising the chance of failure. As Saras Sarasvathy puts it: 'effectuators do not seek to avoid failure; they seek to make success happen'[5] – and that could best be done by getting started, building momentum and seeking active feedback, as the exploration approach advocates. Most assistance schemes, however, are designed by professional supporters, not by venturers, so they will reflect professional caution rather than an over-riding desire for success. Instead of suggesting a bold, go-for-it approach, professional (or even official volunteer) business advisers may err on the side of caution when assisting small businesses, and generally proffer risk-averse advice[6] because they would not want to be blamed if something goes wrong. New venture explorers should therefore beware of being swayed by advice which is over-cautious, particularly if it involves market research, which often proves to be unreliable in practice – after all, all ventures have a degree of risk, and success is never guaranteed.

These are some of the differences between the two approaches and between their possible uses, but there are some commonalities. For instance, whichever approach is followed, decisions need to be made on what is going to be offered and how to sell it and on how to produce the offering and price it; and a comparison needs to be made between projected costs and projected income to see if it is likely to be worth proceeding. Legal formalities will also need to be completed. Nevertheless the approaches do differ, and Table 20.1 provides summaries of the differences identified above, together with a few more.

An implication of Table 20.1 is that formal business plans may be of practical benefit for larger scale enterprises and at a stage after start-up – but not for many small new ventures because of their different starting points and resources. It may therefore be logical for many small ventures to use an exploration approach. To illustrate the options Table 20.2 further describes the key advantages and disadvantages to each approach.

Table 20.1 *Comparison of exploration-based and business-plan-based approaches*

| Aspect | Exploration approach | Business plan approach |
|---|---|---|
| Philosophy | It is not prescriptive. It entails being flexible and, through exploration and experience, developing an understanding of the territory and of the progression options. | It is prescriptive. It sets a predetermined path by first researching and developing a business plan which will determine the route to be followed. |
| Attitude | Reality is uncertain – so proceed accordingly with open eyes ready to do what appears to be appropriate as the situation evolves. | The future can be forecast. So first develop a plan and then follow it – trying to do what the plan suggests should be done. |
| Mind set encouraged | Encourages exploration, flexibility and responsiveness: a discovery attitude. | Encourages following a predetermined path: an operational attitude. |
| Environment assumed | Acknowledges that, in reality, the environment is fluid and uncertain. | Assumes an environment which is relatively static or at least predictable. |
| Starting point | Start from where you are. | Start from where the plan says you should start. |
| When to start | Start early, because that way you will feel that you are doing something, you will gain confidence and momentum, you will find out what works and you will see more opportunities. | Only start when you have researched your idea, explored the market, decided what you are going to do, assessed the viability of your proposal and produced a business plan showing how it will be delivered. |
| On finding obstacles | If you have built and maintained momentum it will help you across and/or around obstacles. You may also by then have seen other opportunities. | Follow the plan. If it doesn't work, stop and re-assess. |
| Preparation and planning | Prepare to be flexible. | Plan the venture in detail and then follow the plan. |
| Route followed | Look for routes going in the direction in which you want to go, follow what appears to be the best route – but be open to finding a better one. | Follow the route specified in the plan. |

| | | |
|---|---|---|
| Guidance used | Find an appropriate mentor/expertise. | If the plan is properly made it should be your ultimate guidance. |
| Scale of venture | Exploration is often good for small ventures. | Business plans tend to be helpful for bigger ventures. |
| When to plan | Do appropriate initial reality checks and plans but only produce a formal written plan when you need one; for instance because potential investors want to see one. | Produce a full written plan at the start because that is when (you are told that) you need one. |
| Approach | Assumes a dynamic situation for which the relevant approach is to have a goal/direction and to be able to steer towards it in a changing environment. | Assumes that the situation can be analysed as if it were static and for which the relevant approach is one of reflective dissection and diagnosis. |
| Consistency with the other approach | An exploration-based approach does not deny that a business plan may be helpful, but does not insist that it is always essential at the start, especially as often parts of it, such as realistic sales projects, cannot be prepared until later. | Business-plan-based approaches usually only cover the components of the traditional business plan and ignore the other key aspects of start-up, which are covered by the exploration principles. |
| Resource and cost considerations | Invest the minimum amount of resource needed and don't put at risk on a venture more than you can afford to lose. But also consider what you will lose if you don't proceed. | Business plans can be relatively expensive to produce – both in time and money. They also encourage the investment of the amount of resource the plan suggests is required and is justified by the expected return. |
| Feasibility | An exploration approach can be followed at any stage – not just at start-up but also pre-start-up and during later enterprise development. | A business plan often cannot realistically be completed at the start-up stage – for instance because not enough is known about the product and its reception in the market. |
| Completeness | The ten principles cover the most important considerations for start-ups. | The standard business plan does not cover some important considerations for start-ups – such as not putting at risk more than you can afford to lose and the importance of gaining momentum. |

Table 20.2 *The advantages and disadvantages of exploration-based and business-plan-based approaches*

| | Exploration approach | Business plan approach |
|---|---|---|
| Advantages | - It is natural – because it is practical and fits in well with evolved instincts.<br>- It works – it is what expert entrepreneurs do.<br>- It is a better preparation for unforeseen obstacles and the reality of an uncertain future.<br>- There is logic to it.<br>- It does cover the key considerations.<br>- It is flexible.<br>- It is cheap(er). | - It provides a straightforward, clear and apparently logical way forwards.<br>- It helps the instigator to assess what to do.<br>- It helps to communicate the main points of the venture to others – and in particular to prospective funders.<br>- It is widely used and supported by many authorities.<br>- Many supporters and/or funders will ask for it in any case. |

Disadvantages

- The approach seems rather uncertain and there's no clear path set out.
- It does not conform to established practice because other people may expect, or want, a business plan at the start.
- It does not insist on the discipline of thinking through actions beforehand and so it does not help new venture explorers to spot potential obstacles.
- It does not provide the information that prospective funders or other supporters may expect to get.
- It isn't (necessarily) the best way.
- It is based on a sales forecast which, at this stage in a business, isn't likely to be reliable – because you can't know how the market will react until you actually get started.
- Following a pre-determined plan can encourage you to be inflexible and less open to new opportunities.
- The effort of producing a business plan leads to an inclination to stick to the chosen path, both because that has been the focus of attention and because so much work has been invested in its determination.

Thus, while the earlier comparison in Table 20.1 suggests that the exploration approach may be more suitable for small new ventures and that formal business plans may be of more practical benefit for larger later-stage enterprises, that is not an absolute rule. Neither approach is suitable for all situations and each approach has its advantages and disadvantages. Thus a small new venture seeking funding may find it helpful to prepare a business plan in order to provide prospective funders with the sort of information they expect, while a larger established business may still benefit from an openness to unforeseen opportunities and a willingness to look for them and respond to them when they do arise. Each should therefore be used when most appropriate and, if the limitations of each approach are understood, the dangers of being led blindly by only one approach can be avoided.

---

Summary of the Key Points of Chapter 20

- A comparison between business-plan-based and exploration-based approaches indicates that they are not straight alternatives. They each have advantages and disadvantages.

- If both approaches are understood, each can be used when it is most appropriate and the dangers of blindly following only one approach avoided.

# 21
# Some Reflections and Implications

> **The Essence of This Chapter**
>
> - The exploration-based approach, with its ten principles, and the business plan approach arc like two tools with different applications – so sometimes one will be the best one to use and sometimes the other.
>
> - For many new small venture start-ups the exploration approach will often be better than a business-plan-based approach.
>
> - The business-plan-based approach appears to be very consistent with the use of the left side of the brain – and for maximum effectiveness both sides of the brain are needed.
>
> - Those who seek to advise and assist such start-ups should recognise this and adjust their methods accordingly.

This book does not present a choice between planning and not planning. Nor does it say that new venture explorers should never plan. What it does suggest is that for many people who are starting new enterprises, planning in the form of the traditional business plan is not appropriate. It also suggests that, because new ventures have a lot in common with exploration, they would be helped by a set of new venture exploration principles.

However, the two approaches are not straight alternatives. As the comparison in Chapter 20 shows, they each cover things that the other does not. In causal thinking (the business plan approach) the fixed point is the specified objective and the focus therefore is on establishing the best means by which to achieve it. In effectual thinking (which is behind the exploration approach) the fixed point is where to start, which is based on what the new venture explorer is and has (in terms of things like ideas, skills, contacts and experience) and on what the venture could afford to lose. The focus then is on exploring what can be done from that starting point to achieve the benefits that the new venture explorer desires. These benefits may not, however, be fixed in advance and what is desired may change as the venture proceeds and new possibilities/opportunities are revealed. This is a process of exploration and is what many explorers do. Some may have looked for a route to particular destination – Columbus was looking for a route to Japan – while others have sought a specific natural resource, such as deposits of gold. All, however, stood to benefit if they were open to other possibilities that their explorations might reveal. Thus, in causal terms, Columbus might be said to have failed because he did not get to Japan, but in effectual terms he succeeded because he revealed to his backers in Spain, and to others in Europe, the potential benefits of the Americas, including its stocks of gold.

The business plan approach does have some advantages, and those listed in Table 20.2 are very relevant. Nevertheless, often a business plan cannot realistically be completed at the start-up stage because not enough is known about the venture and its reception in the market place. Also, the standard business plan does not include all the issues relevant for a new venture to consider and it can encourage a somewhat blinkered approach of following a predetermined route instead of actively seeking out the best one. The exploration approach does offer an alternative to the business plan as a guide for start-ups. It recognises the reality of new venture starts and seeks to highlight the key considerations without being prescriptive. It focuses on achieving goals rather than applying means.

A business plan is frequently required by funders (who don't appreciate its limitations), and it may be a useful format for later development planning once more is known about the reality of the idea and its market. However, although this review suggests that it is often not suitable for many small start-up ventures, not only is it suggested by many as appropriate planning for early-stage ventures – and thus advocated as an essential action for all start-ups – but the business plan is also often viewed as a guide to, and/or indication of, all the key considerations for a new enterprise – and thus used as the basis for new start-up training guides, manuals and courses. This book contends that it is not suitable for either purpose. It is not an appropriate form of planning and it does not usually include or recognise a number of considerations which are very relevant for new ventures.

Thus the criticism of the business plan is not that it includes things that are wrong for ventures/businesses (although it is suggested that some of them are not relevant and/or not practical at an early stage), but that, as a guide to what to do, which is how it is often seen, it does not include some important things that are right for many ventures/businesses and that it can encourage the wrong mindset.

The exploration approach is not perfect either. It is not a straight replacement of the business plan, the ten principles are not a sequential procedure to follow, and the approach is not guaranteed to work. However, the principles do recognise the reality facing many new venture starts and they do include important considerations which are not in the business plan or in any such agenda based on it.

If it is accepted that 'going for it' is more likely to get results then, for those whose aim is success, an exploration approach will often be better. In contrast, for those for whom avoiding failure is seen as being more important than maximising the chance of success, insistence on first doing a business plan is likely to be preferable. In summary, the exploration approach suits, and encourages, a true go-for-it attitude which, it can be argued, is more likely than caution to lead to success – whereas a business plan facilitates caution, and is therefore advocated by those whose prime concern is to avoid failure.

This analysis indicates that, whilst each approach may have its advantages and disadvantages, the approach chosen could be largely determined by the size and stage of the venture. For many people starting a relatively small business, an exploration approach would be more natural, logical and effective than the business-plan-based alternative – and an exploration/effectuation approach would also be appropriate for many non-business ventures.[1] A business plan may be more helpful for larger, more complex, and possibly later stage ventures, for which more detailed planning is appropriate, or when a business plan is being sought by potential external funders.

## Illustration 21.1    Summary of comparison

> The conclusions drawn from the comparison in Chapter 20 might be summarised as follows:
>
> - Neither the exploration approach nor the business-plan-based approach is perfect. They each have strengths and weaknesses.
>
> - Although business plans are frequently advocated by funders and other professional advisers, they encourage a rather blinkered approach and do not cover some of the important issues recognised in the ten principles.
>
> - The business plan method suits those who are cautious, whereas the exploration approach suits those who want to get results.
>
> - Business plans may be more helpful for larger, later stage and more complex ventures, but for new small ventures the exploration approach will often be more suitable and therefore more helpful.

This chapter looks at some of the implications arising from the comparison and at some of the lessons that might be drawn from that analysis.

## TWO TOOLS

What is the underlying requirement for the venture – to achieve a success or to avoid a failure? A cautious business-plan-based approach may be better for avoiding failure, which will of course be best secured by not proceeding, whereas a responsible go-for-it exploration approach may have to accept the risk of failure but, by proceeding, is more likely to lead to success. A conclusion from the comparison may be that for new small ventures, the exploration-based approach is often the more suitable approach. However, it is not necessarily a choice between one and the other. The two approaches are not completely exclusive and, in practice, because both approaches have some advantages, they should be selected, as appropriate, for different situations or stages.

One way of viewing the two approaches could be to liken the exploration approach to a general-purpose tool which is applicable to many aspects of life, including business. In contrast, a business plan is like a special-purpose tool which is applicable to some, but not all, situations within business. It is better, therefore, to use the general-purpose tool first and only to apply the special-purpose tool in situations where its use is relevant and effective. As Saras Sarasvathy says:

> I do not teach effectuation as the only way to do entrepreneurship. Instead the course is built around the notion of two toolboxes – causal and effectual – and how to use them effectively in the creation of new ventures. ... It is important to re-emphasize here that the point of exploring contrasting perspectives ... is not to prove one superior to the other, but to learn to understand and use both.[2]

Therefore in both cases, to gain maximum benefit from the tool, it is important to understand its strengths and weaknesses and know when it is best to use it. Neither is a universal tool, always suitable in all circumstances. The exploration approach may be the tool with a wider range of uses: a bit like a Swiss Army knife. It includes relevant considerations which the business plan misses, and it is often likely to be the more appropriate tool, although not guaranteed to work. The business plan, it is suggested, is a more specialist tool. It does have its uses and is needed when funders demand it. Therefore it should not be ignored, but it should not be recommended as an all-purpose tool and the only tool to use – which has often seemingly been the case. A possible implication of this is that because many people are only taught about the specialist tool and are encouraged to use it, they tend to use it in all situations, including those for which it is not helpful and for which the general-purpose tool would be much more appropriate.

### When to Use Each 'Tool'

Because it is about exploration and not specifically about business, the exploration approach is a suitable tool to use in a wide variety of situations, including, but not limited to, business. Thus if what you are doing in some way involves the exploration of possibilities the exploration principles may be helpful.

Because of the way it has been promoted, the business plan has been elevated to a position of hegemony as a start-up tool. But many people realise that they cannot produce a realistic business plan until they have been in business for a year or two, because before that they don't know enough about, for instance, their market and its potential and receptiveness to their offering. Thus any sales forecast will not be credible and that is why, for such people, an exploration-based approach is appropriate. In contrast, the business plan approach starts with the production of a business plan and the business is not initiated until the market has been investigated, the prospects evaluated and the plan completed and assessed. In exploration you don't do that – but that doesn't mean that you should never plan. If you want support from someone else, especially financial support, you may need to produce a business plan because it is the accepted, and often expected, way of communicating the potential of your ideas and the benefits they might provide for others.

Thus, even for people following an exploration approach, the business plan should not be rejected completely. It can still have its uses, but should be seen as a tool, not an end in itself – the context of which is not fixed but which should be adapted as appropriate. It is, however, a somewhat specialist tool for a relatively limited range of business situations. The activities with which the business plan tool can help include:

- Decision making by the business owner and by prospective business funders.
- Communication with stakeholders, including especially (potential) funders – such as banks, venture capitalists and support/grant agencies.
- A basis for diagnosing problems.
- Learning some of the principles of the proposed business.
- Providing a guide for action.

## TWO SIDES OF THE BRAIN

Another possible implication arising from the comparison of the two approaches is that they arise from different types of thinking and different balances of use of the two different sides of the brain. According to Iain McGilchrist, recent research has suggested that some of the earlier conclusions about the division of the brain are wrong – for instance language is not the sole preserve of the left hemisphere nor visual imagery of the right.[3] Nevertheless, it is clear that the brain is divided and that there are important differences between the two hemispheres, not least because it is helpful to have access to two different types of thinking:

> Survival requires the application of two incompatible kinds of attention to the world at once. A bird, for example, needs to pay narrow-beam sharply focussed attention to what it has already prioritised as of significance – a seed against a background of grit or pebbles, or a twig to build a nest. At the same time, it must be able to bring to bear on the world a broad, open, sustained and uncommitted attention, on the look-out for whatever else may exist. Without this capacity it would soon become someone else's lunch while getting its own. Birds and animals all have divided brains, and regularly use one hemisphere for vigilant attention to the world at large, so as to make sense of it, including to bond with their mates, and the other for the narrow attention that enables them to lock onto whatever it is they need to get. Humans are no different in this respect: we use our left hemisphere to grasp and

manipulate, and the right to understand the world at large and how things within it relate to one another, as well as our relationship with it as a whole.[4]

The left hemisphere, it is suggested, tends to work on models, not reality, because models are much clearer and abstract, and so from them it is relatively easy to provide the analysis needed to decide on concrete actions. The left hemisphere tends to achieve this clarity and attention to detail by excluding from the models everything that doesn't fit. In contrast, the right hemisphere sees the world as changing, evolving and inter-connected – but not fully knowable. To manipulate the world, it has been said, we need the left hemisphere – to understand it we need the right.[5]

These differences are echoed in the differences between a business-plan-based approach, with a focus which amounts to constructing and then following a model, and the effectuation-influenced exploration-based approach, with its emphasis on an awareness of, and the need to react to, the evolving situation in the real world. It is of interest to note McGilchrist has suggested that 'we are living in the West in a culture dominated by the take on the world of the left hemisphere'[6] and:

> The nature of the attention we choose to pay alters the nature of the world we experience, and governs what it is we will find. This in turn governs the type of attention we deem it appropriate to pay. Before long we are locked into a certain vision of the world, as we become more and more sure of what it is we see. To a man with a hammer everything begins to look like a nail.

And some beautiful research demonstrates that what we do not expect, we just do not see.[7]

Hence McGilchrist's efforts to redress the balance (referred to in Chapter 19 above) and reassert the relevance of the right hemisphere:

> The left hemisphere is manifestly not in touch with reality, and when it does not understand something it simply makes up a story that makes sense in its own terms and tells it with conviction. It prioritises as 'truth' the internal consistency of a system rather than its correspondence with the world outside the window. It tends to deny problems, abjure responsibility and take an unreasonably positive view of itself and its capacities.[8]

Is there a reflection of that in the theme of this book? If we have come to rely too much on the left hemisphere and excluded the right, have we also, in a similar way, come to put too much faith in the business plan to the exclusion of a wider awareness of, and reaction to, reality as it emerges in unpredictable ways?

However, as McGilchrist insists, we do need, and should therefore use, both hemispheres:

> One way of looking at the difference would be to say that while the left hemisphere's raison d'être is to narrow things down to a certainty, the right hemisphere's is to open them up into possibility. In life we need both. In fact for practical purposes, narrowing things down to a certainty, so that we can grasp them, is more helpful. But it is also illusory, since certainty

itself is an illusion – albeit, as I say, a useful one. Similarly the right hemisphere appreciates that all things change and flow, and are never fixed and static as the left hemisphere sees them. Nor are they isolated and atomistic (left hemisphere), but reciprocally interconnected (right hemisphere).[9]

## SOME IMPLICATIONS

Essentially this book is about the implications to be drawn from a look at new venture start-ups which goes beyond the business plan. Instead of viewing new ventures as early stage business which might have a bit in common with explorations, it considers new ventures to be a form of exploration which might at some stage develop into a business – and therefore the key implication is that for many new venture explorers the ten exploration principles will be more suitable than a business plan. Further observations are made throughout the book about the relevance of some of the points raised and from them various other lessons might be drawn. Therefore to try to list all the other possible implications would be to repeat much of the book. Instead, this chapter concludes by offering a summary of some of them:

- Although some people may consider a business plan to be the best format for assessing the potential of a business venture, that does not mean that it necessarily includes the key considerations for such a new venture – and this book suggests instead that it ignores many of them.

- There is an alternative to the traditional business-plan-based approach, and the best approach depends on the circumstances. These different approaches also suit different attitudes to goals. Nevertheless, for many start-ups, an effectuation-based exploration approach may often be the better way.

- Those who don't start their new venture with a business plan should not feel that they are dissenters or exceptions to the rule. Many people feel that they cannot produce a realistic business plan until they have been in business for a year or two, because before that they don't know enough, for instance about their market and its receptiveness to their offering. The exploration approach acknowledges this.

- Start-up teaching for new venture explorers should not try to force the business plan approach onto people in circumstances for which it is not appropriate.

- Similarly enterprise advice does not have to, and should not, simply follow a business-plan-based menu. Even if a full business plan is not advocated, relying on business plan thinking encourages a reliance on activities such as market research, which may be misleading, and pre-determined plans, which may be misguided. It does not cover key things like how to proceed in uncertainty, the relevance of looking for other opportunities, the benefit of gaining momentum and the importance of social capital.

- Because of the different philosophies and different methods of thinking encouraged and/or required for the different approaches, business supporters should consider the impact that a preferred approach can have upon the development of the entrepreneurial person as well as the entrepreneurial venture. Providing advice which is more appropriate should lead to more business success.

---

Summary of the Key Points of Chapter 21

- A comparison between business-plan-based and exploration-based approaches indicates that they each have advantages and disadvantages.

- However, the two approaches are not straight alternatives. They have been likened to two tools with different applications.

- The exploration approach is more like a general-purpose tool with relatively wide application. In contrast the business plan is like a specialist tool which is more appropriate in some situations.

- The business-plan-based approach may rely on, and/or encourage, an over-dependence on left-brain thinking instead of a more balanced use of both hemispheres.

- A key implication from the analysis is that, for many new small venture start-ups, the exploration approach will often be better. Therefore those who seek to advise and assist such start-ups should recognise this and adjust their methods and thinking accordingly.

## 22
# Postscript – The Relevance of Exploring

> The Essence of This Chapter
> - It reinforces the message that new ventures are a form of exploration.
> - It emphasises key implications of an exploration approach to new venturing.
> - It highlights the relevance of the ten principles as a guide for new venture explorers.

The book is about and for those people who are thinking of launching a new venture and a useful starting point is not to think of a new venture automatically as an early stage business, even if it is also acknowledged that it has something in common with exploration. If a venture is labelled as a business the tendency will be to introduce too much business thinking and received business wisdom at too early a stage – and, as Part I shows, such thinking is often largely based on big business understanding and is not appropriate for many new ventures. Instead, most new ventures should be considered to be a form of exploration which might, at some stage, develop into a business.

One of the reasons for thinking of a new venture as a form of exploration is that the future is uncertain.

We may try to predict what will happen based on extrapolations from current trends, but history shows us that discontinuities are the norm, not the exception, and it must be expected that some unforeseen, and unforeseeable, events and outturns will occur. To borrow an effectuation analogy (see Illustration 4.4, p. 45), the future is not like a jigsaw puzzle, in which a picture of what the finished work will be like can already be revealed and all that is then necessary is to put the pieces into place. Instead, it is much more like making a collage of found pieces where the overall trend or intention might be apparent but where the final result will depend on the nature of the pieces discovered during the making process.

According to Charles Handy, successful entrepreneurs have an average of nine failures for every success, and oil companies expect to drill nine empty wells for every one that flows. A key aspect of exploration is that explorers expect to have to test a number of approaches before they can identify one that is at least reasonably productive. That is why they can't produce maps or plans before they have explored the territory. In this situation, finding a route that does not work, or a test drill that doesn't produce oil, is not a failure but a step towards finding an area that does work. Indeed, if no other approaches are tried, how is it possible to know that the chosen route or site is indeed the best?

A failure is often viewed as something that could have been prevented with the right preparation – but picking the right route or location in an unknown situation is not something that can be done without exploration, so it is not a failure to find that the first route tried doesn't work or otherwise isn't the best way. It is of course possible with a degree of common sense to rule out some potential sites or routes as likely to be in an unproductive place or going in the wrong direction, and thus reasonably certain not to work – but it is not possible to demonstrate in advance which one will work. That is what exploration is about.

If failure implies that something went wrong in a way that should have been prevented by better preparation, it implies that someone is at fault in not doing that preparation. That is what the business plan approach tends to suggest. It is based on the assumption that market research can predict consumer response and thus, if the plan based on that research does not work, it encourages a belief that there must have been an avoidable fault in its preparation or execution.

Illustration 22.1   Creating unnecessary failure?

> An implication of taking an exploration approach is that explorers know that not every avenue explored will be successful, and finding which avenues are dead-ends is a necessary part of any exploration process. However, because a business plan approach insists on a plan for each avenue to be tried, each try becomes a separate venture and so, if one doesn't work, it becomes a failure. The business plan therefore leads to more people thinking they have failed. Also, because it can encourage inflexibility, the use of a business plan in inappropriate situations may put barriers in people's minds, making them less prepared to look for, deal with or take advantage of the unexpected and thus also more likely to fail.

Therefore another message from this book is that, in new ventures, finding an approach that does not work is not a culpable failure, but is instead an important part of finding what does work. However, because this exploration takes place in unknown situations, finding routes that don't work is always a possibility, which is why the principle of not putting at risk more than you can afford to lose is very relevant. But the key message remains – don't demotivate yourself or others by unnecessarily labelling as a failure what is a normal part of the exploration process.

This difference in outlook, which the exploration-based and business-plan-based approaches encourage, is symptomatic of an important difference of perspectives, to which recent studies of the different hemispheres of the brain would appear to be relevant. Those who have studied this aspect of the brain have found that left hemisphere thinking tends to be useful for quick decision making in the area of the expected because it has a narrow focus, applies logic and uses models, whereas right hemisphere thinking applies a broad awareness to spot, see the implications of, and react to, the unexpected.

A business plan process produces a model and then encourages a narrow focus on implementing it. It is thus very consistent with left-hemisphere thinking. If market research works then the future can be predicted and the unexpected eliminated – so a narrow focus on implementing the model should work efficiently. In reality it does sometimes succeed, but is it often more by chance than judgement, and instead the plan often has to be changed or abandoned because of the unexpected.

Instead, proceeding by looking broadly for unforeseen opportunities, or obstacles, and then being ready to react to them appropriately, is the nature of exploration and is much more consistent with right hemisphere thinking. If a lesson of history is that the future is rarely a simple extrapolation from the present and that the unexpected often happens, then a wider scanning of reality is needed. In this situation a narrow, 'logical', model-based, left-brain focus, based on spurious market research, may at times succeed but is generally not the best way to proceed into an uncertain future.

This does not mean that new venture explorers should never use their left hemispheres. Some aspects of a venture do require a narrow focus on detail and a conformity with standards but, as suggested above, other aspects need a right hemisphere approach. Therefore combining a narrow approach for things like managing money and following legal requirements and regulations with a broader lookout for, and openness to, new developments is the best recipe for success. So the explorer should be aware when left hemisphere thinking is appropriate but should not follow it to the exclusion of the right hemisphere – which, like it or not, is what has been encouraged by an over-reliance on the business plan. If it is accepted that the future is uncertain, then proceeding accordingly by maintaining a wide awareness on the lookout for both possible threats and possible opportunities – and a readiness to react to them – is much more sensible than narrowly trying to implement a model based on unreliable research.

It has been suggested that the thinking of many people who are entrepreneurial does tend to be dominated by their right hemispheres. As the business plan is something which is very formalistic, logical and sequential, and therefore very compatible with left-brain thinking, it could potentially be helpful as a way of balancing people who are predominantly using their right hemispheres. However, if McGilchrist is right and in the West the left hemisphere has become the dominant way of thinking, then for many people a business plan will just reinforce a lack of balance and not redress it. Thus the ten principles are deliberately designed to facilitate, if not actually to encourage, right hemisphere thinking – in order to balance a left hemisphere tendency. Also, for the same reason, this book deliberately avoids lots of technical detail and instructions, for instance on the legal form of business or financial systems, which are the sort of things that a left hemisphere approach likes and looks for.

So, the key message of this book is that exploration is a valid way to describe the essence of a new venture but that successful exploration requires not the rigid following of a predetermined path, but an openness to new possibilities which are only likely to be revealed once the venture is under way. Thus the book does not prescribe a detailed process or sequence of activities but instead seeks to encourage and support an appropriate way of thinking by offering some principles to guide that exploration. This, it suggests, is more suitable for most new ventures than simply trying to follow a business plan. Therefore the advice to a new venture explorer is to try to explore the optimal route to your goal by following the principles and not doing a business plan until it is appropriate and/or necessary to secure the support of others.

### Summary of the Key Points of Chapter 22

- A new venture should not be thought of as an early-stage business which has something in common with exploration, but should be seen instead as a form of exploration which might, at some stage, develop into a business.

- Successful exploring requires, not a narrow focus on a predetermined route, but a wide openness to new emerging possibilities.

- Exploring is thus consistent with right brain hemisphere thinking – and should help to balance any over-reliance on left hemisphere thinking, such as a business plan can encourage. Both hemispheres need to be used, but the left should not predominate.

- An exploration approach, guided by the principles recommended in this book, should thus be very suitable for many new ventures.

# Part IV
# Further Information
# 23 Supplementary Information

This part of the book provides supplementary information on a number of issues or aspects of enterprise potentially relevant for new venture explorers. In some cases the aspect is mentioned or alluded to earlier in the book, but in a situation where providing fuller information about it might interrupt the flow of the relevant chapter. In other cases the issue is not mentioned earlier, but some people might nevertheless have expected to see it – so it is outlined in this section together with reasons for its earlier omission. The issue/aspects are:

- Behavioural economics
- Causation and effectuation
- Caution – and proceeding cautiously
- Legal structures
- New venture terminology
- Social capital
- Social enterprises
- Traits
- Additional aspects
    - Elevator pitch
    - Idea + Know-How + Know-Who

Market research

Mentors

Sales forecasts in business plans

The starting point

## BEHAVIOURAL ECONOMICS

Behavioural economics could be said to be based on the belief that people behave as they do rather than as theory might suppose that they behave. In traditional economics, for instance, the assumption has been that people behave rationally – for instance basing their purchasing decisions on a logical analysis of which is the best product for them from the choice on offer. As a result, such an invariably rational person has been even referred to as *homo economicus*.

However, psychologists and others began to point out that often people did not do what might have been supposed to be the logical thing and were influenced instead by other factors. The new economics foundation (nef) has distilled this alternative thinking into seven principles:

1. 'Other people's behaviour matters.

2. Habits are important.

3. People are motivated to "do the right thing".

4. People's self-expectations influence how they behave.

5. People are loss-averse.

6. People are bad at computation.
7. People need to feel involved'.[1]

Thus, for instance, people are often influenced more by the behaviour of others than by logic – as seems to be the case in the drinking and smoking practices of young people. People often do things from habit, rather than from conscious decisions, but they also do some things because they think they ought to do them, such as giving blood and giving dinner parties, which they might do less readily if they were offered money for them. If people have made a commitment to do something they are likely to continue to do it even if is no longer logically the best thing for them to do. Also, people generally put more effort into avoiding a loss of something they have than they would into gaining the same thing if they didn't have it.

Thus people do not invariably take the rational path that maximises their self-interest. Instead, human behaviour is complex – and it is in that environment that new ventures are built. They are likely to work better if they recognise this.

### CAUSATION AND EFFECTUATION

Effectuation and causation are introduced in Chapter 4 (see Illustration 4.4), but more information about them is provided here because they are important concepts. The terms were introduced by Saras Sarasvathy who has examined how successful entrepreneurs operate.[2] She researched the methods used by a sample of entrepreneurs who had taken their business to the stage of stock market flotation, and found that they took the future as fundamentally unpredictable yet controllable through human action. Therefore they started from a basis of who they are (their traits, tastes and abilities), what they know and who they know and, because the future is uncertain, they started small and used the means closest at hand to move directly into action without extensive prior research. For the same reason they did not commit more than they could afford to lose but, through their actions, they discovered other possible means and/or stakeholders (suppliers, customers, investors, collaborators) and, being flexible, they altered their actions to incorporate and/or use them as and when appropriate. Eventually some of the emerging effects coalesce into goals and a method of operating that are both achievable and desirable – and this is the stage at which a formal business plan might be prepared and formal investment sought.

That is the process Sarasvathy has called 'effectuation'. The alternative is a causation approach which, she suggests, would start with a pre-agreed business plan and then try to follow it carefully, investing what the plan suggests is necessary and justified by the projected returns. In contrast, effectuation sees the future as essentially unpredictable, although possibly to some extent controllable and, in an unpredictable environment, progress is best made by moving forward in the desired direction from a basis of what is possible now, while not committing more than one can afford to lose at any stage and being open to new opportunities for processes, markets and/or partners as they present themselves:

> Causation processes take a particular effect as given and focus on selecting between means to create that effect.

Effectuation processes take a set of means as given and focus on selecting between possible effects that can be created with that set of means.

**Illustration 23.1   The Principles of Effectuation**

According to Read *et al.* 'there is a science to entrepreneurship – a common logic ... observed in expert entrepreneurs across industries, geographies, and time. The underlying principles are ... simple and easy to put into action [although they] challenge and even invert traditional logic used in mature organizations'[3] Those principles can be summarised as:

1. *Start with your means (the bird-in-hand principle)*: Don't wait for the perfect opportunity. Start taking action, based on what you have readily available: who you are, what you know, and who you know – your experience, your knowledge and your contacts.

2. *Set affordable loss (the affordable loss principle)*: Evaluate opportunities based on whether the downside is acceptable, rather than on the attractiveness of the predicted upside – make decisions based on what you can afford to lose rather than only on what you might gain.

3. *Leverage contingencies (the lemonade principle)*: Embrace surprises that arise from uncertain situations. The unexpected is likely

to happen and cannot be avoided – so be prepared to take advantage of it when it does happen. Remain flexible rather than being tethered to existing goals.

4. *Form partnerships (the crazy quilt principle)*: Form partnerships with people, such as suppliers or customers, who self-select and can and want to make a real commitment jointly to create the future with you. Don't worry so much about competitive analyses and strategic planning.

5. *Create opportunities (the pilot-in-the-plane principle)*: When you can, make the future happen by working with things within your control and with people who want to help co-create it. Then you don't need to worry about predicting the future, determining the perfect timing, or finding the optimal opportunity.

*Source*: Based on S. Read, S, Sarasvathy, N. Drew, R. Wiltbank and A.-V. Ohisson. *Effectual Entrepreneurship* (Abingdon: Routledge, 2011).

Learning a language is an example of an activity better done effectually rather than causally. Trying to learn all the rules first and then to work out all the grammar and vocabulary before attempting to utter a sentence generally leads to hesitation and a sense of increased difficulty. Attempting to speak something in a language as soon as possible and before you are certain about everything provides a sense of achievement and generates feedback – and picking up a language that way is the best route to fluency. Thus learning a language is about getting started and then learning rather than learning and then getting started – it is about learning by doing, not learning then doing.

## CAUTION AND PROCEEDING CAUTIOUSLY

If you want to cross a dark room, do you first spend time trying to find a torch or do you just feel your way along at a pace which allows you to stop in time if you feel an unexpected obstacle? Doing the latter may actually be quicker.

If it has snowed and you need to walk along the road to the nearby shop, do you get a shovel and clear the snow so that you can see where the path is, or do you just proceed cautiously to the shop? If you clear the path first then you and other people can then proceed quickly along it, but if you are the only person likely to use the path then clearing it first will take much longer than walking carefully to avoid slipping.

If you wanted to lead a large group of people through a piece of unknown territory then, indeed, you might want to reconnoitre a route first before you come back to lead the group across. However, if you are the only traveller, then surely you would just try to cross it once? An initial one-person reconnaissance is worth doing prior to taking a lot of people down the route. But if there is only one person travelling does it still make sense to try it once and then, if you do succeed in finding your way to the destination, leaving it to return only to do it again? And if the first route doesn't work you try another – because for one person, to reconnoitre is to travel.

## Proceeding with Caution

These examples suggest that there are many situations in life when you have to operate in conditions of uncertainty and when, although it might be possible to try to reduce the uncertainty through research, the effort required to do that would be as much, if not more than, the effort required just to proceed cautiously.

Similarly in a new business venture: many people, when starting their businesses, don't think that they know enough about the likely demand for the product or service, or about the potential performance of the business, to be able to complete a standard business plan. Theory suggests that they should therefore carry out market research but, particularly for a small business, the sort of market research that might help would amount to, or would need to be on a similar scale to, actually starting the business. As Principle 5 says, the only reliable test is a real one – so prior research on a lesser scale is not going to produce reliable results. The cheaper, quicker and no more risky way is often not to conduct extensive prior testing, but to proceed cautiously – and also following Principle 2 and not committing more than the venture can afford to lose.

## Caution without Proceeding

It is thus sensible advice in an unknown situation to proceed with caution. However in new venturing there are times where undue caution can be harmful – and that can be the case with professional advice. It has been suggested that professional (or even official volunteer) business advisers, and many official supporters, may err on the side of caution when assisting small businesses, and generally proffer risk-averse advice.[4] If something done on the basis of their advice and/or support were to go wrong their reputation might suffer and if, as a banker or support agency, they had advanced a loan or grant, they might be blamed for their actions. Therefore in general they might be more concerned to avoid failure than to see a particular venture succeed. For the same reason, therefore, they are more likely to favour the business plan approach, because that provides a more detailed analysis of what could go wrong and thus more opportunity to advise caution.

Such advisers are likely therefore to shy away from the 'rock-climbing' approach, which believes that, if you really want to do it, then getting started is more important than exhaustive investigation. That is particularly the case when investigation involves market research which often proves to be unreliable in practice. Therefore beware of excessive professional caution – it can harm your prospects.

## LEGAL STRUCTURES

Possible legal structures for a new venture do not feature in the ten principles. Nevertheless they are an important consideration for anyone starting a new venture which needs to operate and deal with others on a legally recognised basis. To enter into binding contracts with others (which the other partners to an agreement might require) some form of legally recognised existence is necessary which makes it clear who, if anyone, can be held liable for the actions of the venture.

The two main choices for a venture are whether it should be given its own separate legal identity or whether it should merely operate as an activity for which the person, or people, behind it can automatically be held personally responsible, including being responsible for any debts or obligations it incurs.

### Limited Company

One of the most obvious and common forms of separate legal existence is a properly registered limited company. Such companies are recognised as distinct entities in law and are described as limited companies because the responsibility of the people who set them up and/or control them is limited. In the case of companies limited by shares the owners' liability is limited to the amount contributed as share capital and the shareholders together own the business and can receive dividends from its profits in proportion to the number and type of shares they hold. Alternatively, liability can be limited by guarantee. A business limited by guarantee is controlled by its members, who each agree to guarantee its liabilities up to an agreed amount (in the UK often £1 each) but who cannot benefit from the distribution of the profits of the business. A company limited by shares can be a public or a private company depending on whether the invitation to subscribe for the shares is open to the public or restricted in certain ways.

However, there is generally a bit more to the responsibility than that because the directors of a company, who are appointed by the shareholders or members to direct the affairs of the company, have an obligation to run the company responsibly and could, in some circumstances, be held personally liable for its debts.

Establishing a limited company involves a process of defining aspects of the business's operation (which are then specified in its Memorandum and Articles of Association) and registering it officially. Incorporation in this way imposes obligations such as registering the directors of the company and submitting annual accounts. Similar separate legal existence can, in the UK and for organisations which qualify, also be conferred through registration as an Industrial and Provident Society, for which there are slightly different annual reporting obligations.

Another variation in the UK is a Community Interest Company (CIC), which is registered as a company but with the declared intention of addressing (some of) the needs of a particular declared community. A CIC can be limited either by shares or guarantee, but limits are imposed on the amount of dividend or other distribution of assets to members or shareholders.

### Organisations without Limited Liability

*Sole Trader.* In business terms, operating as a sole trader is the simplest form of structure. An individual can start a business in this way with the minimum of fuss. In this situation, however, there is no legal distinction between the assets of the business and those of its owner. People who are sole traders are 'self-employed' and their earnings as a business are subject to income tax. They are thus fully liable for any debts or obligations of the business.

*Partnership.* A business can also be established as a partnership of a group of individuals doing business together. However, the business does not have a separate legal identity, and each partner is jointly and severally liable for any liability incurred by the partners acting for the business. The liability of the partners is unlimited, except in the case of the (so far less common in the UK) 'limited partnership'. Thus many advisers suggest avoiding partnerships of two people in which each is liable for all that the partnership does but neither has a controlling interest for resolving disputes.

*Unincorporated ventures.* Another common form of organisation, often established in default of doing anything else, is an unincorporated body. A lot of clubs and societies operate in this way. They can have bank accounts, employ people and in other ways take on contractual obligations – but the people held to be legally responsible for the actions and obligations of the organisation will be the members of the management committee or other controlling group. They will each be individually liable for the debts and actions of the organisation.

**NEW VENTURE TERMINOLOGY**

As Illustration 1.2 indicates, there is a varied and sometimes conflicting vocabulary in use to refer to aspects of new venture creation. The following notes are therefore offered as a quick guide to some of the terminology that might be encountered.

*Business* is defined in the *Oxford Handy Dictionary* as 'task, duty; thing that is one's concern; habitual occupation; serious work; thing(s) needing dealing with; difficult matter; process, affair, structure ...; action on theatre stage; buying and selling, trade; commercial house, firm'.[5] However, when people refer to *a business* it is generally the 'buying and selling, trade, commercial house, firm' bit of that definition that covers their meaning. They also generally think that such an activity is undertaken for the financial gain of the person or people who own the business. Sometimes, especially with smaller businesses, the person who owns the business is also the person who runs or manages it – and who is sometimes thus referred to as an *'owner-manager'*.

Businesses can be any size, from the very small one-person business up to giant multinational businesses. However, there is a significant division between small and large businesses. It is not possible to specify exactly at what point a growing *small business* changes to become a *large businesses*, but a popular category for categorisation is the *small and medium-sized enterprise (SME)*, which is often agreed to be up to 250 employees. However, it appears that somewhere between 50 and 100 employees is the limit over which it is possible for one person to exercise informal control in any form of organisation. Thus small businesses below this limit generally have top-down structures and informal systems, control by direct supervision and sometimes a lack of objectivity, whereas larger businesses behave differently, with formal organisation structures, systems and decision making and objective strategies and planning. Thus small businesses are not mini versions of large businesses: they behave differently and often need to be treated appropriately.

An *enterprise* can also refer to a business, but sometimes also to an endeavour or organisation which does not trade and might not be considered by many people to be a business. Thus it can be a more acceptable label for those who think business is primarily about making as much money as possible, sometimes even by underhand means. A *venture* also generally has the same wider enterprise meaning, which is why it is the term often used in this book.

An *entrepreneur* in its original use in an economic context was someone who engaged in an economic activity at risk. Whereas a landlord could fix a rent in advance and an employee could agree his or her wage in advance, someone like a shopkeeper had to buy goods without necessarily knowing what the demand for them might be, and a farmer had to invest in growing crops without knowing what price they might fetch. Thus the word *entrepreneur* came to be attached to someone who ran a business. However in some people's view it has become associated with an undue focus on personal profit. The 'Gombeen man' in Ireland, the 'Del Boy wheeler dealer' in the UK or the person 'who wants to make a quick buck' in the USA typify what the word has come to mean for some people – as chancers and/or gangsters. That is not a fair description of many entrepreneurs but the association sometimes persists, which is why the word *venture* is preferred in this book – and because it can apply to more enterprises than just those that are strictly businesses.

*Entrepreneurship* refers to the activity of being an entrepreneur, but it does also seem on occasion to refer to an attitude or approach that might be deployed not just in running a business, but also when working in an enterprise for someone else. Thus being *entrepreneurial* can mean the same as someone who is enterprising, and not just someone who starts and/or runs a business.

Working for someone else is referred to as *employment* and working on your own for yourself as *self-employment*, even if you then undertake work for others on a sub-contract basis. However, it was only when formal long-term contracts of employment came in that this distinction arose. Until then there was little to distinguish a window cleaner, who was hired for as long as it took to clean the windows in question, from a labourer who worked for a long time for the same employer but was actually re-hired every day and had no more security of employment than the window cleaner.

*Creativity* is also associated with being enterprising and/or entrepreneurial – because they involve the creation of something new, such as a new activity, product or service, or doing something in a new way or in a new market. Creativity is also associated with *invention* and *innovation*. The difference there, however, is that while invention involves devising something new, innovation is often taken to mean the exploitation of new ideas to produce something usable and useful.

## SOCIAL CAPITAL

As Mark Earls has put it: 'The influence of others is to be found in every aspect of our lives, in the big and the small things we do. We cannot escape it; even if we pretend we are superior and highly principled and self-determining, we all do it all of the time. We are Super Social Apes'.[6] New ventures are made and run by people and, as Earls indicates, people are socially connected. In the context of a new venture, social capital is about the potential and uses of those social connections and their relevance to the start-up, and running, of an enterprise. Such connections have always been important, but this has not always been recognised and, for instance, they have not been acknowledged in classical economics or listed among the requirements for a successful enterprise. Now, however, the impact of interpersonal links is receiving more recognition.

For instance, over 25 years ago Peterson and Rondstadt[7] produced the formula: 'Entrepreneurial Success = Entrepreneurial Idea + Entrepreneurial Know-How + Entrepreneurial Know-Who' which was a relatively early recognition of the importance of social connections in building a business. It uses the term 'know who' and the same idea has also been referred to by the term 'networking' and aligned, more recently, with the concept of social capital. However, our understanding of social capital is still evolving and Schuller *et al.* have commented that 'the relative immaturity of social capital as a concept ... (and its) rapid proliferation has allowed a diversity of approach' and that 'social capital has several adolescent characteristics: it is neither tidy nor mature; it can be abused, analytically and politically; its future is unpredictable; but it offers much promise'.[8]

Despite the lack of a uniform understanding of social capital, this book nevertheless uses that term. Not only does no better alternative seem to be available, but the term is helpful because the word 'social' highlights the social nature of the connections in question and the word 'capital' suggests that, like financial capital, it is something which needs to be acquired before it can be used and is not inexhaustible.

## The Capitals Necessary for Enterprise

The formula from Peterson and Rondstadt is one list of the key requirements for an enterprise. Traditionally, however, other key 'factors of production' were thought to be necessary for a business, such as raw materials, labour and (financial) capital. This concept can be traced back to Adam Smith, although he referred to the 'component parts of price' which he considered to be land or natural resource, labour, and 'capital stock' such as tools, machinery and buildings.[9]

These factors are now sometimes labelled 'capitals', and, since Smith's day, other factors have been suggested for inclusion in the list. Thus manufactured resources are now sometimes called 'fixed' or 'physical capital', or 'working capital' if they consist of stocks of finished or part-finished goods. Labour is referred to as 'human capital' and 'financial capital' is recognised as the money invested, or available for investment, in the business. And to this list 'social capital' has also been added as a key requirement.

For instance when the UK Department for International Development (DFID) sought to understand the factors relevant to 'sustainable livelihoods' it produced the model which included human capital, social capital, natural capital, physical capital and financial capital. Recently other capitals have also been suggested as necessary for enterprise such as 'knowledge capital' and 'intellectual capital'; with the former referring to the skills and knowledge of how to do things that the people employed in a business can bring to their work and the latter to ideas and copyrights and patents which help to protect them from use by other businesses.

## A Short History of Social Capital

When Hanifan first introduced the concept of social capital in 1916 he used it to refer to the community involvement which he, as a state supervisor of rural schools and educational reformer, identified as important for successful schools.[10] However, it wasn't until the term was used by people like Bourdieu, Coleman and Putnam that it gained greater currency.

Bourdieu thought of social capital as the connections that helped people to position themselves in social space, for which the power and resources that could be accessed through social capital were very relevant. Thus he defined social capital as 'the aggregate of the actual or potential resources which are linked to possession of a durable network of more or less institutionalized relationships of mutual acquaintance or recognition'.[11] He connected social capital to both cultural and material economic assets and to links between individuals, between institutions, and between individuals and institutions. This suggests that it has two dimensions:

- First, it is a resource that is connected to group membership and social networks and the volume of social capital possessed by an individual depends on the size of the network created; and

- Second, it is about the quality of these relationships and especially the capacity of the groups to mobilise resources in their own interests.[12]

Coleman's early research on schools and schooling helped shape government policy on racial integration in the USA. For him social capital was connected to social networks which have value in increasing individual and group productivity and also to physical capital in the form of tools and human capital in the form of education. According to him social capital:

> Is defined by its function. It is not a single entity, but a variety of different entities having two characteristics in common: They all consist of some aspect of social structure, and they facilitate certain actions of individuals who are within the structure[13]

Social capital was then the subject of a World Bank research programme in the 1990s but arguably it gained its greatest recognition from the work of Putnam. In his influential book *Bowling Alone*,[14] which was published in 2000 following an earlier article with the same name, he claims to have found a decline in the social capital of America in the second half of the last century – a trend which he suggests has significant implications for everyone in America. Putnam talks of social capital as 'social networks and the associated norms of reciprocity [which come] in many different shapes and sizes with many different uses'[15] and refers to a growing body of evidence that such civic connections 'make us healthy, wealthy and wise'.[16] Social capital, he suggests:

- 'Allows citizens to resolve collective problems more easily.'

- 'Greases the wheels that allow communities to advance smoothly.'

- 'Widens our awareness of the many ways in which our fates are linked.'[17]

The importance of social capital has been recognised also in the context of business and entrepreneurship. A number of commentators have pointed out, for instance, the relevance and importance of social contacts and networks to entrepreneurship and, in the introduction to a special issue of the *International Small Business Journal* devoted to the relationship between social capital and entrepreneurship, Cope *et al.* stated that:

> The presence or absence of social capital is likely to influence the very nature of the entrepreneurial venture. Social capital involves social interaction and would appear to reside in and between connections to others. It could even be regarded as representing 'networking capital' since in essence it is really a relational phenomenon and a term that actually refers to the social connections entrepreneurs use to obtain resources they would otherwise acquire through expending the human or financial capital.[18]

## What Is Social Capital?

Despite the definitions quoted above it is not easy to specify the nature of social capital. A key question is whether social capital is essentially one thing or several separate things. Putnam, for his book *Bowling Alone*, proposed and applied a method for measuring the amount of social capital in each of the American states and from this produced a one dimensional comparative scale. He did this by combining 'fourteen indicators of formal and informal community networks and social trust (because they) are in turn sufficiently intercorrelated that they appear to tap a single underlying dimension'[19] – an approach which suggests that different aspects of social capital can indeed be added together to contribute to a single meaningful total. Putnam then used this scale to indicate a correlation between the level of social capital and aspects of the fabric of social life such as the level of crime, the level of child welfare, the equality of income distribution and the level of civic equality. Thus, in order to show the effects of social capital, Putnam assumes the validity of a single dimensional index as if all aspects of social capital ultimately contribute to the same effect. In that case each variety of social capital must either be fungible – that is capable of mutual substitution – or be so closely linked to other varieties of social capital that they are interdependent.

In his book *Outliers* Malcolm Gladwell comments on an investigation into the reason why the inhabitants of the town of Roseto in Pennsylvania have had significantly better levels of health than the USA as a whole, including having roughly half the average death rate from heart disease. The conclusion was that this difference was not due to factors such as diet or exercise, because they didn't differ from the norm for the area, but was instead due to the nature of the relationships within the community, which were still like those of the town in Italy from which the ancestors of many of the town's residents had once come. In other words, Roseto's social capital was the factor that made its citizens healthier.[20] For Gladwell therefore, as for Putnam, social capital can be viewed as a common factor in civic engagement and interpersonal relationships.

However, in *Bowling Alone* Putnam acknowledges that this is not always the case when he describes the differences between bonding and bridging social capital because he states that 'some kinds of bonding social capital may discourage the formation of bridging social capital and vice versa'.[21] Also, in the introduction to *Democracies in Flux*, written together with Goss, after alluding to the debate about whether physical capital was sufficiently homogeneous to be added up in a single ledger, he comments that 'a dentist's drill, a carpenter's drill, and an oil rigger's drill are all examples of physical capital, but they are hardly interchangeable'.[22] He and Goss then state that: 'The same is true of social capital – it comes in many forms that are useful in many different contexts, but the forms are heterogeneous in the sense that they are good only for certain purposes and not others'.

Others have also suggested that there are different and non-interchangeable forms of social capital. For instance, Smith has concluded that, although 'the notion of social capital is a useful one in evaluating the resources to be found in a place' it is 'totally impossible and probably misguided to reduce the concept of social capital in its many varied forms to a single measurable index',[23] and Coleman suggested that:

> like physical capital and human capital, social capital is not completely fungible, but is fungible with respect to specific activities. A given form of social capital that is valuable in facilitating certain actions may be useless or even harmful in others.[24]

Although the example of Roseto suggests that more social capital leads to better health, this may not always be the case. According to Campbell: 'health-related behaviours, such as smoking, diet, condom use, and exercise, are determined not only by conscious rational choice by individuals on the basis of good information, as traditional health educational approaches assumed, but also by the extent to which broader contextual factors support the performance of such behaviours'.[25] In other words those health-related behaviours are socially influenced in that, for instance, we tend to smoke less if there is general social disapproval of the habit of smoking. However, in this case what matters is not just the overall amount of social contact, as in the case of Roseto's health, but whether that social contact approves of smoking or not. Thus adding a set of social contacts who disapproved of smoking to a set of contacts who approved of, or at least tolerated, smoking, would not double this effect of social capital, but would tend to cancel it out. The two sets of social capital would not each be interchangeable with each other.

### Different Forms of Social Capital

If social capital comes in different forms, what are they? Putnam identified two dimensions (or components) of social capital: bonding and bridging, and linking was then suggested as a third dimension. Fukuyama named his book *Trust*[26] after one aspect of social capital and the Conscise project suggested six headings in attempt to encapsulate the key parts of other definitions:

> Social capital consists of resources within communities which are created through the presence of high levels of ...:
> 
> - Trust.
> 
> - Reciprocity and mutuality.

- Shared norms of behaviour.
- Shared commitment and belonging.
- Both formal and informal social networks.
- Effective information channels.[27]

And, in an enterprise context, it has been suggested that there are several different forms of social capital[28] including those to be found in:

- Contact within the local and close community.
- Contact outside the local community.
- Sources of relevant information.
- Trust and vouching.
- Encouragement of specific behaviours.

### An Analogy with Vitamins

One way of thinking about the nature of social capital, at least in the context of its relevance to enterprise, might be through an analogy with the different components of food. It is generally acknowledged that, at least for humans, a healthy diet needs to include protein, carbohydrates, fats and sugars, and this can be likened to an effective enterprise mix for which social, physical, human and financial capitals are all necessary. If the amount of social capital in the enterprise or development mix can meaningfully be presented as a single total then it might be like protein in the food mix, because, although protein is available from a number of different animal and vegetable sources, in terms of their contribution to diet these forms are more or less interchangeable and therefore it is relevant to include them all in measuring the total amount of protein present.

If, however, there are different forms of social capital that are not substitutable, then it is not like protein. Instead, following the example of Halpern,[29] Bridge has suggested that a comparison with vitamins offers a better analogy for the effects of social capital.[30] Vitamins are important in their contribution to diet, but the different vitamins have different and very specific effects and adding more of one vitamin is no substitute for the lack of another. Also, once enough of a particular vitamin is present, adding more will not add any extra benefit.

Other aspects of the vitamin analogy which might have parallels for the application of social capital to enterprise are:

- The need for vitamins only became apparent when food was 'purified' or processed in some way, for instance to preserve it for long ocean voyages, which removed the vitamins present in fresh food. Could attempts to provide impersonal, and thus unbiased, economic assistance have the effect of separating such provision from the social capital that used to accompany a more personal involvement?

- Once the existence and relevance of vitamins became established it took some time before all the relevant vitamins were identified and their sources established.

- Some vitamins are generated naturally in a healthy human body living in the right conditions, and do not normally need to be supplemented.

- Having too much of a particular vitamin can be harmful. In this context it is interesting to note a conclusion of Pirolo and Presutti[31] who looked at the influence on start-ups of two aspects of social capital, which they called 'strong ties' and 'weak ties', and found not only that their effects were separate, but also that, in some circumstances, too much 'close and strong social networking can negatively influence the ability of start-ups to reach high levels of innovation performance'.

Illustration 23.2   The importance of social 'rules'

> William Baumol suggests the extent to which entrepreneurship is applied to productive business depends more on society's 'rules' than on the supply of entrepreneurs. He looks at historical evidence from ancient Rome, early China, the Middle Ages and Renaissance Europe. In ancient Rome, he suggests, 'people of honourable status had three primary and acceptable sources of income: landholding, usury and political payments'. Productive commerce and industry could generate wealth but not prestige, so those who wanted prestige directed their entrepreneurship to the acceptable applications which helped the individual concerned but were unproductive for society as a whole. In Medieval China also the 'rules' did not favour productive entrepreneurship and instead accorded supreme prestige to high positions in the state bureaucracy, thereby encouraging the application of entrepreneurship

> to unproductive activity. In England in the early Middle Ages the practice of leaving estates to the eldest son meant that often the only opportunity for the younger sons of barons lay in warfare, with the result that their entrepreneurship became destructive.
> Under all these systems, entrepreneurship was not necessarily lacking but was often directed by society's 'rules' to unproductive or destructive applications. However, in situations like that in England at the time of the Industrial Revolution, when the 'rules' had changed to allow those who engaged productively in industry to accumulate not just wealth but also respect and influence, the application of entrepreneurship to productive purposes was encouraged and the economy benefited.
> 
> *Source*: based on W. J. Baumol, 'Entrepreneurship: Productive, Unproductive, and Destructive', *Journal of Political Economy*, 1990, vol. 98, no. 5. pt.1.

### Why Social Capital Is Important for Enterprise

An enterprise may require financial, human and physical capital to operate but to start, to survive, to prosper and even to grow, it needs the many things that a network of interpersonal connections can bring, such as ideas, guidance, support, information, encouragement, credibility, sponsorship, customer contact, references and introductions – for instance to possible new suppliers and/or partners. Therefore it has been identified as one of the essential components in the enterprise mix.

In other words, contacts with people can be helpful – so cultivate them for two-way benefits.

## SOCIAL ENTERPRISES

If your venture is considered to be a business, or at least to have an economic impact, then it will be considered to be part of the economy and therefore to belong in one of its sectors. Economies are said to be about apportioning resources and, it has been suggested, the two main means for apportioning resources are the market and the state. Traditionally economists have therefore identified two sectors in an economy: the public sector and the private sector.

The public sector administers and implements the wishes of the state. It includes government departments, local authorities and other public bodies which provide services such as defence, policing, health and education on an overall or needs-based basis and which get the funding they require ultimately from some form of taxation. The private sector includes those businesses which are privately owned and which generally provide goods or services by trading them to people or organisations which are able and willing to pay for them. They do this in order to make a profit for their backer and their funding comes from the customers they find in the market place.

However, it is increasingly being recognised that there is a wide range of organisations that appear to be in neither sector: which are neither trading to make money for distribution to backers nor using taxpayer funds to do public good. They include charities and churches, associations and amateur clubs, foundations and fair trade companies, cooperatives and community bodies, mutuals and trades unions, voluntary organisations and professional bodies. Although many of them are enterprises, because they are generally not formed primarily to make a profit for their members and/or founders, they are not considered to be in the private sector. And although many of them have social purposes, because they are not part of the government system, paid for by taxes, they are not considered to be in the public sector. Being therefore in neither of the two sectors traditionally ascribed to an economy, they are sometimes referred to jointly as the third sector.

As many of these enterprises have a social purpose, they are often referred to as social enterprises or community enterprises. As such, like private sector enterprises, they have to generate enough income to survive and therefore managing them has a great deal in common with managing private sector businesses. The only difference is that the people running social enterprises want them to survive in order to deliver some social (or environmental or moral) good rather than just to make more money.

Many definitions have been offered for social enterprises. Bridge *et al.* have compared some of these definitions and found that 'there is little that they all agree is an essential criterion except that of having a social purpose'. Even the re-investment of profits is not always an absolute requirement as some definitions do allow some profit distribution. However, they suggest,

> the definitions, in general, do suggest that there are some coherent traits, values and organisational formats which mark out social enterprises, and the social economy of which they

are a significant part, as a distinctive economic, social and cultural sphere of activity.[32]

Bridge *et al.* also suggest that in reality there is no clear dividing boundary between private sector and social enterprises and in particular few clear distinctions between some of the smaller enterprises in each sector. The corollary of this is that starting a new enterprise is not significantly different depending on whether it is seen to be in the private or the third sector – and either is likely to be helped by the principles advocated in this book.

## TRAITS

Traits are discussed here because they have been proposed as an explanation of why some people are more enterprising or entrepreneurial than others. This theory implies that the kind of person you are will influence whether you become an entrepreneur. However, it is now generally accepted that the link between such traits is complex or that trait theory is obsolete. For instance, it is clear that most entrepreneurs do not possess all the traits listed below, and that there are many people who do possess them but who would not be described as entrepreneurs. In practice, therefore, if you want to start a business don't worry too much about what traits you have.

### An Outline of Trait Theory

According to trait theory there is a set of traits that characterise an entrepreneur and are predictive of entrepreneurial behaviour. Such traits are supposed to include:

*Achievement motivation:* Entrepreneurial people have a strong need for achievement (sometimes labelled NAch).

*Risk-taking propensity:* While they must be able to countenance risk, enterprising people are not high risk-takers – instead they seek to manage and/or to minimise it. (See also the section on entrepreneurs and risk in Chapter 14.)

*Locus of control:* Entrepreneurs want to be in control of events.

*Need for autonomy:* Entrepreneurs like to be in control of their own destiny, rather than being dependent on others.

*Determination:* Entrepreneurial people also possess determination.

*Initiative:* An entrepreneurial individual may also need to be proactive and able to take the initiative to seek and utilise openings and opportunities.

*Creativity:* The essence of entrepreneurship is to bring something new into being – thus this is linked to innovation.

*Self-confidence and trust:* Entrepreneurs have confidence in themselves and seek to be confident in others.

## Critiques of Trait Theory

Simple trait theory implies that the kind of person you are will influence whether you become an entrepreneur. It therefore assumes that entrepreneurship is derived more from nature than nurture. However, a review of traits suggests that the connection between innate qualities and entrepreneurship is not simple. The traits and qualities described above do impact on behaviour, but it is accepted that most entrepreneurs do not possess all the enterprise traits identified, and many of the traits are also possessed by those who would not be described as entrepreneurs. Among the authors who have specifically commented on this are:

> Frédéric Delmar[33] suggests that trait theory has significant limitations. He argues that there is a little consistency in trait research and evidence linking predisposition, enterprise and performance is at variance. In effect, a particular combination of traits does not predict a particular form of behaviour.

Scott Shane also distrusts the trait approach and comments that:

> entrepreneurial activity is episodic. Because people engage in entrepreneurial behavior only at particular points in time, and in response to specific situations, it is impossible to account for entrepreneurship solely by examining factors that should influence all human action in the same way all of the time.[34]

Elizabeth Chell has explored this approach in some detail, for instance in her book on *The Entrepreneurial Personality*.[35] A fundamental problem, she explains,

> is to arrive at an understanding of the nature of personality in general, given the considerable revisions in thinking that have taken place in recent years. ... The question of what is 'personality' and what is the basis of the trait construct are fundamental to such concerns. The lay person uses the term 'personality' in a very different way to that of the psychologist. ... Thus, when the lay person uses the term 'entrepreneur' they are referring to a type; they can 'recognise one when they see one' because they believe that they have sufficient public information to label that individual as an entrepreneur: This is not the same, clearly, as the scientific process that a psychologist engages in – the ability to isolate traits that are predictive of specific behaviours; in this case it is the belief that there is a trait or set of traits that characterise an entrepreneur and are predictive of entrepreneurial behaviour.[36]

In theory personality traits should help to predict behaviour in a variety of different situations. Thus if individuals who cheat on their income tax are dishonest and have a dishonesty trait, that should lead them to be dishonest in other situations – but research has not found this to be the case and people who do cheat on their taxes do not also appear to be more likely than non tax-cheats to be dishonest in other situations. Also, personality traits might be supposed to be linked to attitudes, but attitudes assessed through questionnaires do not seem to correlate with observed behaviour.

**In Summary**

Thus it would seem that in terms of an understanding of enterprise and entrepreneurship, traits have been something of a red herring. Some traits may be ascribed to those exhibiting enterprising behaviour, but in general traits do not seem to apply in all situations, and attitudes, which might be supposed to be based on traits, do not seem to be linked to behaviour. Further, while some traits may be identified in those who are enterprising, those who are enterprising do not all appear to have all of those traits – and some of those that do have some or all of the traits do not appear to be enterprising. For a new venture explorer it is thus probably best to ignore traits and to get on with it.

## ADDITIONAL ASPECTS

### Elevator Pitch

The idea behind an elevator pitch is that it is a description of your venture which you could give to a potential customer, supporter or, investor if you happened to get into a lift (called an elevator in the USA) with them and needed to explain your idea before they got out again. While that scenario may not happen in quite that way, being ready for it entails identifying the key features of your offering which are likely to attract the interest of other people and then establishing how to communicate them in a short message. It thus forces you to analyse what you are offering and why other people might like it and, once you have worked that out, you will be ready to build your customer and support base.

**Idea + Know-How + Know-Who**

Twenty-five years ago Peterson and Rondstadt produced the formula (alluded to in Chapter 10):

> *Entrepreneurial Success = New Venture Idea + Entrepreneurial Know-how + Entrepreneurial Know-who.*[37]

For a relatively complex process such as starting a business it is not possible to indicate every relevant consideration in one simple formula but this attempt probably comes as close as any. It has the advantages both of highlighting three important key areas and of not highlighting money as a key issue, although many people act as though it is the main factor.

The three key issues it does highlight are:

- *New venture idea.* The idea is the starting point which, it is suggested in Part I under 'where' to start a business, should be based on where you are in terms of your experience, abilities (know-how) and contacts (know-who).

- *Entrepreneurial know-how.* You will need both appropriate know-how for your idea (which is why it is best to choose an idea based on what you do know) and for your business activity. The latter includes things like being able to sell and to look after money. So, if you don't have those skills, try to learn them and/or get others who do have them to help you.

- *Entrepreneurial know-who.* Know-who is an issue which has often been overlooked in official advice but its importance is now being recognised. It has been referred to as 'networking' but increasingly it is been considered as an aspect of social capital, which is itself being recognised as an essential component in the economic mix.

## Market Research

'The findings obtained from most market research are completely unreliable. ... [However] the notion that risk can be mitigated by soliciting consumer opinion is so tempting that millions of pounds continue to be spent pursuing it. And yet it's regularly reported that over 80% of new product launches fail.'[38] The reason why so much market research is unreliable is that often people do not know what leads them to behave in the way they do. But, because they are guided by subconscious influences, they will invent logical reasons if asked, often without realising it (see Illustration 18.1). Thus simple market research of the sort that might be done for a business plan is often unlikely to produce a meaningful result. The sort of research that does work is observing how consumers behave when actually presented with the opportunity to purchase the product or service for real. But, for a small business, that can involve the same amounts of work as actually starting the business. So why spend time or money on separate research if it costs no more to start and see where it takes you?

A business plan, however, requires market research to produce the sales forecast which will be the foundation for its projections. The unreliability of much market research means that many business plans will be built therefore on sand.

*Sales Forecasts (in Business Plans)*
At the heart of a business plan there is a sales forecast because, without that, it is not possible to make any financial projections about the business, such as production costs and sales income. Unfortunately, it is also the source of many of the problems associated with the business plan approach. For instance:

- Many people starting a new business feel, quite rightly, that they cannot produce a realistic sales forecast.

- A sales forecast will depend on market research in some form, and market research, especially for new businesses, is very unreliable. The sales forecast is likely, therefore, to be the weakest part of the business plan, yet it is the bit on which many other parts depend. The sales forecast therefore probably means that the business plan is more like a house of cards than a reliable dwelling.

- Whatever sales forecast is used will set limits on the business. The sales forecast will be used to determine not just the likely sales income, but also what size of production facility is required, what level of staffing that indicates, what premises are needed and what level of overheads. They, in turn, will determine the investment needed. Thus, because of a forecast which is probably unreliable, the business is established with specific dimensions which also set limits to the expectation and ambition of the people concerned. Those dimensions will thus determine the scale of the business and, although they can, of course, be changed, there will be a cost involved. If, for instance, the sales projections turn out to be over-optimistic and the business has too much production capacity, premises that are too big and/or too many staff, the cost of reducing that may be more than a new business can stand. If, on the other hand, the projections are too low, then the opportunity for doing more business will be missed until new investment can be found for bigger capacity.

**The Starting Point**

When does a business 'start'? Those who advocate the business plan as the essential starting point for a new business enterprise seem to assume that anyone launching the business will have a definite intention to establish a new formal full-time business with a distinct product or service for which there is a clearly identified market. Therefore it will also be possible to determine things like costs and prices, ownership and organisation structures, and financing requirements, and thus complete all the main parts of a business plan and then hopefully raise the finance required before the business formally starts.

But how many start-ups actually conform to that mould? The case study on Illustration 1.1 is based on a real situation, but at what stage in the case might it be said that the business really started? Was it when the first enquiry was received, when the first piece of work was delivered, when the first payment was received, when the instigator first registered himself as self-employed, when he felt sufficiently confident in the future of the business to stop scanning the jobs section of the local paper, or when the business was formally converted into limited company? And at what point could a credible business plan have been completed with a realistic assessment of the business's service offering, its pricing structure, its marketing needs, and the likely resultant demand for it work? (The founder of the business in question cannot say at which particular point the business really started and reflects that it was only after he had been operating for a couple of years that he would have felt that he knew enough about his market and service offering to have been able to complete a credible formal business plan, had he thought it was necessary or helpful to have one.)

# Notes

## 1 THE PURPOSE OF THIS BOOK

1. L. Hunter speaking at a University of Ulster seminar on 'Developing a strategy and vision for social entrepreneurship', Coleraine, 10 September 2007.

## 2 BUSINESS PLANS – WHY ARE THEY ADVOCATED?

1. HSBC, 2011. *Quick Start Business Plan* Available at: www.tsbc.co.uk/sbo/hsbckn/viewlesson.aspx?lid=35 (accessed 31 January 2011).

2. Barclays Bank, *A Guide to Writing a Business Plan*, No.004, July 2009 www.barclays.co.uk/startup support (accessed 16 November 2012).

3. P. Burns, *Entrepreneurship and Small Business* (3rd edition) (Basingstoke: Palgrave, 2011) p. 365.

4. D. Deakins and M. Freel, *Entrepreneurship and Small Firms* (5th edition) (Maidenhead: McGraw Hill, 2009) p. 316.

5. Harvard Business School Press, *Creating a Business Plan* (Boston, MA: Harvard Business School Publishing, 2007), back cover.

6. Business Link, *Prepare a Business Plan*, on www.businesslink.gov.uk (accessed 6 July 2010).

7. Invest NI advertisement on a hoarding at Belfast City Airport, October 2011.

8. Go for It, www.goforitni.com/business-planning (accessed 21 November 2012).

9. A. A. Gibb, *Towards the Entrepreneurial University: Entrepreneurship Education as a Lever for Change* (National Council for Graduate Entrepreneurship Policy Paper 003, May 2005).

10. R. S. Edwards and H. Townsend, *Business Enterprise: Its Growth and Organisation* (London: Macmillan, reprint 1967).

11. E. Penrose, *The Growth of the Firm* (Oxford: Oxford University Press, 1959) p. 19.

12. E. Penrose, *The Growth of the Firm* (Oxford: Oxford University Press, 1959) p. 19.

13. It appears to be logical if viewed from inside the professionals' world – but not necessarily from outside that world.

14. See Note 13.

## 3 ARE BUSINESS PLANS APPROPRIATE?

1. J. E. Lange, A. Perdomo and W. D. Bygrave, 'Do Actual Outcomes Justify Writing Business Plans either for Educating Students or for Starting Real Ventures?', presentation to *6th AGSE Conference* (Australia: Adelaide, 2009).

2. A. T. Tjan, R. J. Harrington and T.-Y. Hsieh, *Heart, Smarts Guts and Luck* (Boston, MS: Harvard Business Review Press, 2012) p. 11 (stress in original).

3. H. Mintzberg, *The Rise and Fall of Strategic Planning* (Hemel Hempstead: Prentice Hall, 1994) p. 97.

4. J. Brinckmann, D. Grichnik and D. Kapsa, 'Should Entrepreneurs Plan or Just Storm the Castle?', *Journal of Business Venturing*, Vol. 24, 2010, p. 24.

5. J. Cornwall, *The Entrepreneurship Educator Newsletter*, June 2010.

6. B. Bjerke, *Understanding Entrepreneurship* (Cheltenham: Edward Elgar, 2007) p. xiii.

7. G. D. Meyer, 'The Reinvention of Academic Entrepreneurship', *Journal of Small Business Management*, Vol. 49 No. 1, 2011, p. 1.

8. S. Blank, 'Why the Lean Start-Up Changes Everything', *Harvard Business Review*, May 2013, p. 67.

9. D. Kahneman, *Thinking, Fast and Slow* (London: Penguin Group, 2011) p. 218.

10. P. Graves, *Consumer.ology* (London: Nicholas Brealey Publishing, 2010) dust jacket.

11. P. Graves, *Consumer.ology* (London: Nicholas Brealey Publishing, 2010) p. 4.

12. P. Graves, *Consumer.ology* (London: Nicholas Brealey Publishing, 2010) p. 18.

13. Quoted in H. Mintzberg, *The Rise and Fall of Strategic Planning* (Hemel Hempstead: Prentice Hall, 1994) p. 7.

14. J. K. Galbraith, *The Affluent Society*, (first published in USA 1958) 4th edition (London: Penguin, 1991) p. 6.

## 4 BUSINESS PLANS ARE NOT THE ONLY OPTION

1. P. Bissell and G. Barker, *A Better Mousetrap: A Guide for Innovators* (3rd edition) (Halifax: Wordbase Publications, 1993).

2. www.wendykennedy.com (accessed 20 November 2012).

3. E. Ries, *The Lean Startup: How Constant Innovation Creates Radically Successful Business* (London: Penguin, 2011).

4. S. Read, S. Sarasvathy, N. Drew, R. Wiltbank and A.-V. Ohlsson, *Effectual Entrepreneurship* (London: Routledge, 2011).

5. S. D. Sarasvathy, *Effectuation: Elements of Entrepreneurial Experience* (Cheltenham: Edward Elgar, 2008) p. 21.

6. S. D. Sarasvathy, *Effectuation: Elements of Entrepreneurial Experience* (Cheltenham: Edward Elgar, 2008) p. 24.

7. Based on: S. D. Sarasvathy, *Effectuation: Elements of Entrepreneurial Experience* (Cheltenham: Edward

Elgar, 2008) pp. 15/16 as summarised in Table 11.1 in S. Bridge and K. O'Neill, *Understanding Enterprise, Entrepreneurship and Small Business* (Basingstoke: Palgrave, 4th edition 2013) p. 238.

8. S. D. Sarasvathy and S. Venkataraman, 'Entrepreneurship as Method: Open Questions for an Entrepreneurial Future', *Entrepreneurship Theory and Practice*, Vol. 35 No.1, 2011.

## 5 ENTERPRISE AND EXPLORATION

1. H. Koning, *Columbus: His Enterprise* (London: Latin America Bureau, 1991) on back cover.

2. P. Burns, *Entrepreneurship and Small Business* (3rd Edition) (Basingstoke: Palgrave, 2011) p. 365.

3. P. Lunn, *Basic Instincts* (London: Marshall Cavendish, 2008) p. 42.

4. J. K. Galbraith, *The Affluent Society*, (first published in USA 1958) 4th edition (London: Penguin, 1991) p. 6.

5. M. Earls, *Herd: How to Change Mass Behaviour by Harnessing Our True Nature* (Chichester, UK: John Wiley & Sons Ltd, 2009) p. 162.

6. M. Earls, *Herd: How to Change Mass Behaviour by Harnessing Our True Nature* (Chichester, UK: John Wiley & Sons Ltd, 2009) p. 123.

7. D. Brooks, *The Social Animal* (London: Short Books, 2011) p. 108.

8. K. Popper, 'Of Clouds and Clocks', in *Objective Knowledge* (Oxford: Oxford University Press, 1973).

9. J. Lehrer, 'Breaking Things Down to Particles Blinds Scientist to Big Picture', *Wired Magazine*, April 2010 (www.wired.com/magazine/2010/04/st_essay_particles) (accessed 19 March 2012).

## 6   A GUIDE FOR EXPLORERS?

1. A. A. Gibb, *Towards the Entrepreneurial University: Entrepreneurship Education as a Lever for Change* (National Council for Graduate Entrepreneurship Policy Paper 003, May 2005).

## 7   THE STARTING POINT: UNDERSTANDING HOW TO EXPLORE

1. Reported on www.thomasedison.com/guotes.html (accessed 3 February 2013).

2. Reported on www.thomasedison.com/guotes.html (accessed 3 February 2013).

## 8   PRINCIPLE 1 – AN ENTERPRISE IS A MEANS NOT AN END

1. L. Hunter speaking at a University of Ulster seminar on 'Developing a strategy and vision for social entrepreneurship', Coleraine, 10 September 2007.

2. J. Masters, *Pilgrim Son: A Personal Odyssey* (London: Michael Joseph, 1971) p. 59.

## 9   PRINCIPLE 2 – DON'T COMMIT MORE THAN YOU CAN AFFORD TO LOSE

1. S. D. Sarasvathy, *Effectuation: Elements of Entrepreneurial Experience* (Cheltenham: Edward Elgar, 2008) p. 24.

## 10 PRINCIPLE 3 – START FROM WHERE YOU ARE

1. 'Entrepreneurial Success = New Venture Idea + Entrepreneurial Know-how + Entrepreneurial Know-who 'from R. Peterson and R. Rondstadt, 'A Silent Strength: Entrepreneurial Know-Who', The 16th ESBS, efmd IMD Report (86/4) p. 11.

## 12 PRINCIPLE 5 – THE ONLY RELIABLE TEST IS A REAL ONE

1. Philip Graves quoted by D. Woodward in 'Big Ideas' in *Director* February 2011 (www.director.co.uk) (accessed 3 February 2011).

2. M. Holbrook and E. Hirschman, 'The Experiential Aspects of Consumption: Consumer Fantasies, Feelings and Fun', *Journal of Consumer Research*, Vol. 9 (September 1982) pp. 132–140.

3. E. Ries, *The Lean Startup: How Constant Innovation Creates Radically Successful Business* (London: Penguin, 2011) p. 1.

4. P. Graves, *Consumer.ology* (London: Nicholas Brealey Publishing, 2010) p. 3.

5. S. Sarasvathy, *Effectuation* (Cheltenham: Edward Elgar, 2008) pp. 171–175.

## 13 PRINCIPLE 6 – GET STARTED AND GET SOME MOMENTUM

1. S. Sarasvathy, *Effectuation* (Cheltenham: Edward Elgar, 2008) p. 90.

2. H. Mintzberg, *The Rise And Fall of Strategic Planning* (London: Prentice Hall, 1994) p. 221.

3. H. Mintzberg, 'Rethinking Strategic Planning Part I: Pitfalls and Fallacies', *Long Range Planning*, Vol. 27 No. 3, 1994, p. 17.

## 14 PRINCIPLE 7 – ACCEPT UNCERTAINTY

1. HM Treasury, *The Green Book* (Norwich: The Stationery Office, 2003) p. 32.

2. J. Rowson and I. McGilchrist, *Divided Brain, Divided World* (London: RSA, February 2013) p. 49.

3. H. Mintzberg, 'Rethinking Strategic Planning Part I: Pitfalls and Fallacies', *Long Range Planning*, Vol. 27 No. 3, 1994, p. 19.

4. US Department of Defense, News Transcript: News Briefing – Secretary Rumsfeld and Gen Myers, 12 February 2002.

5. M. Simon, S. M. Houghton and K. Aquino, 'Cognitive Biases, Risk Perception and Venture Formation: How Individuals Decided to Start Companies', *Journal of Business Venturing*, Vol. 15, 1999, pp. 113–134.

6. S. Read, S. Sarasvathy, N. Dew, R. Wiltbank, and A.-V. Ohlsson, *Effectual Entrepreneurship* (Abingdon, UK and New York, USA: Routledge, 2011) pp. 24/5.

7. Based on: S. D. Sarasvathy, *Effectuation: Elements of Entrepreneurial Experience* (Cheltenham: Edward Elgar, 2008) pp. 15/16.

## 15 PRINCIPLE 8 – LOOK FOR OPPORTUNITIES

1. J. Flaherty quoted in *Keep Calm and Sure It'll Be Grand* (Chichester: Summersdale, 2012).

2. Quoted by J. Dimbleby in *Russia* (London: BBC Books, 2008) p. 21.

3. S. Shane, *A General Theory of Entrepreneurship* (Cheltenham: Edward Elgar, 2003) p. 10.

4. S. Sarasvathy, *Effectuation* (Cheltenham: Edward Elgar, 2008) p. 61.

## 16 PRINCIPLE 9 – BUILD AND USE SOCIAL CAPITAL

1. M. Earls, *Herd: How to Change Mass Behaviour by Harnessing Our True Nature* (Chichester, UK: John Wiley & Sons Ltd, 2009).

2. L. J. Hanifan, 'The Rural School Community Centre', *Annals of the American Academy of Political and Social Science*, Vol. 67, 1916, pp. 130–138.

3. N. Christakis and J. Fowler, *Connected* (London: Harper Press, 2010) p. 111.

4. M. Southon and C. West, *The Beermat Entrepreneur* (Harlow: Pearson Education, 2002) p. 8.

5. E. Parsloe quoted in NESTA, *A Guide to Setting Up a Peer Mentoring Programme* (www.nesta.org.uk) (accessed 2 February 2011).

## 18 FOLLOWING THE PRINCIPLES

1. P. Graves, *Consumer.ology* (London: Nicholas Brealey Publishing, 2010) pp. 31/2.
2. B. Franklin, *The Autobiography, 1791* – taken from J. S. Leo Lemay and P. M. Zall (eds), *Benjamin Franklin's Autobiography* (New York: Norton, 1986) Part I, p. 28.
3. P. Lunn, *Basic Instincts* (London: Marshall Cavendish, 2008) p. ix.

## 19 STRIKING A BALANCE

1. Quoted in H. Mintzberg, *The Rise and Fall of Strategic Planning* (Hemel Hempstead: Prentice Hall, 1994) p. 120.
2. H. Mintzberg, *The Rise and Fall of Strategic Planning* (Hemel Hempstead: Prentice Hall, 1994) pp. 189 and 191.
3. H. Mintzberg, *The Rise and Fall of Strategic Planning* (Hemel Hempstead: Prentice Hall, 1994) p. 323.
4. J. Rowson and I. McGilchrist, *Divided Brain, Divided World* (London: RSA, February 2013) p. 17.

## 20 COMPARING APPROACHES

1. See, for instance, S. D. Sarasvathy, *Effectuation: Elements of Entrepreneurial Experience* (Cheltenham:

Edward Elgar, 2008) and S. Read, S. Sarasvathy, N. Dew, R. Wiltbank, and A.-V. Ohlsson, *Effectual Entrepreneurship* (Abingdon, UK and New York, USA: Routledge, 2011).

2. See, for instance, S. D. Sarasvathy, 'Causation and Effectuation: Toward a Theoretical Shift from Economic Inevitability to Entrepreneurial Contingency', *Academy of Management Review*, Vol. 26 No. 2, 2001.

3. S. D. Sarasvathy, *Effectuation: Elements of Entrepreneurial Experience* (Cheltenham: Edward Elgar, 2008) p. 24.

4. P. Graves, *Consumer.ology* (London: Nicholas Brealey Publishing, 2010), on the dust jacket.

5. S. D. Sarasvathy, *Effectuation: Elements of Entrepreneurial Experience* (Cheltenham: Edward Elgar, 2008) p. 17.

6. K. Mole, 'Gambling on Growth or Settling for Survival: The Dilemma of the Small Business Adviser', *Journal of Small Business and Enterprise Development*, Vol. 7 No. 4, 1990, pp. 305–314.

## 21 SOME REFLECTIONS AND IMPLICATIONS

1. For instance, see S. D. Sarasvathy and S. Venkataraman, 'Entrepreneurship as Method: Open Questions for an Entrepreneurial Future', *Entrepreneurship Theory and Practice*, Vol. 35 No. 1, (January 2011) pp. 113–135.

2. S. D. Sarasvathy, *Effectuation: Elements of Entrepreneurial Expertise* (Cheltenham: Edward Elgar, 2008) pp. 231/2.

3. I. McGilchrist, *The Master and His Emissary* (New Haven and London: Yale University Press, 2010) p. 1.

4. J. Rowson and I. McGilchrist, *Divided Brain, Divided World* (London: RSA, February 2013) pp. 13/14.

5. I. McGilchrist, *RSA Animate – The Divided Brain*, www.thersa.org (accessed 25 October 2011).

6. J. Rowson and I. McGilchrist, *Divided Brain, Divided World* (London: RSA, February 2013) p. 20.

7. J. Rowson and I. McGilchrist, *Divided Brain, Divided World* (London: RSA, February 2013) p. 14.

8. J. Rowson and I. McGilchrist, *Divided Brain, Divided World* (London: RSA, February 2013) p. 19.

9. J. Rowson and I. McGilchrist, *Divided Brain, Divided World* (London: RSA, February 2013) p. 14.

## PART IV  FURTHER INFORMATION

1. E. Dawnay and H Shah, *Behavioural Economics: Seven Principles for Policy-Makers* (London: New Economics Foundation, 2005) p. 2.

2. See, for instance, S. D. Sarasvathy, 'Causation and Effectuation: Toward a Theoretical Shift from Economic Inevitability to Entrepreneurial Contingency', *Academy of Management Review*, Vol. 26 No. 2, 2001.

3. S. Read, S. Sarasvathy, N. Drew, R. Wiltbank and A.-V. Ohisson. *Effectual Entrepreneurship* (Abingdon: Routledge, 2011) p. ix.

4. K. Mole, 'Gambling on Growth or Settling for Survival: The Dilemma of the Small Business Adviser', *Journal of Small Business and Enterprise Development*, Vol. 7 No. 4, pp. 305–314.

5. *The Oxford Handy Dictionary* (London: Chancellor Press, 1986) p. 104.

6. M. Earls, *Herd: How to Change Mass Behaviour by Harnessing Our True Nature* (Chichester, UK: John Wiley & Sons Ltd, 2009) p. 162.

7. Based on R. Peterson and R. Rondstadt, 'A Silent Strength: Entrepreneurial Know-Who', The 16th ESBS, efmd IMD Report (86/4) p. 11.

8. T. Schuller, S. Baron and J. Field, 'Social Capital: A Review and Critique', in S. Baron, J. Field and T. Schuller (eds), *Social Capital: Critical Perspectives* (Oxford: Oxford University Press, 2000) pp. 24 and 35.

9. A. Smith, *An Inquiry into the Nature and Causes of the Wealth of Nations*, 1776.

10. L. J. Hanifan, 'The Rural School Community Centre', *Annals of the American Academy of Political and Social Science* 67 (1916) pp. 130–138 and *The Community Centre* (Boston, MA: Silver, Burdett and Co., 1920).

11. P. Bourdieu, 'The Forms of Capital', in J. G. Richardson (ed.), *Handbook of Theory and Research for the Sociology of Education* (New York: Greenwood Press, 1986) p. 248.

12. F. Sabitini, *Social Capital, Public Spending and the Quality of Economic Development: The Case*

of Italy (Milan: Fondazione Eni Enrico Mattei, 2006).

13. J. S. Coleman, *Foundations of Social Theory*. (Cambridge, MA: Belknap Press of Harvard University Press, 1990) p. 302.

14. R. D. Putnam, *Bowling Alone: The Collapse and Revival of American Community* (New York: Simon & Schuster, 2000).

15. R. D. Putnam, *Bowling Alone* (New York: Simon & Schuster, 2000) p. 21.

16. R. D. Putnam, *Bowling Alone* (New York: Simon & Schuster, 2000) p. 287.

17. R. D. Putnam, *Bowling Alone* (New York: Simon & Schuster, 2000) p. 288.

18. J. Cope, S. Jack and M. Rose, 'Social Capital and Entrepreneurship: An Introduction', *International Small Business Journal*, Vol. 25 No. 3 (2007) p. 214.

19. T. Schuller, S. Baron and J. Field, 'Social Capital: A Review and Critique', in S. Baron, J. Field and T. Schuller (eds), *Social Capital: Critical Perspectives* (Oxford: Oxford University Press, 2000) pp. 24 and 35.

20. M. Gladwell, *Outliers* (London: Allen Lane, 2008) pp. 3–11.

21. R. D. Putnam, *Bowling Alone* (New York: Simon & Schuster, 2000) p. 362.

22. R. Putman and K. Goss, 'Introduction' in R. Putnam (ed.), *Democracies in Flux* (Oxford: Oxford University Press. 2002) p. 8.

23. G. Smith, 'A Very Social Capital: Measuring the Vital Signs of Community Life in Newham', in B. Knight *et al.* (eds), *Building Civil Society: Current Initiatives in Voluntary Action* (West Malling: Charities Aid Foundation, 1998) p. 67.

24. G. Smith, 'A Very Social Capital: Measuring the Vital Signs of Community Life in Newham', in B. Knight *et al.* (eds), *Building Civil Society: Current Initiatives in Voluntary Action* (West Malling: Charities Aid Foundation, 1998) p. 67.

25. C. Campbell, 'Social Capital and Health: Contextualising Health Promotion within Local Community Networks', in S. Baron, J. Field and T. Schuller (eds), *Social Capital: Critical Perspectives* (Oxford: Oxford University Press, 2000) p. 182.

26. F. Fukuyama, *Trust: The Social Virtues and the Creation of Prosperity* (New York: Free Press, 1995).

27. A. Kay, Chapter 6: 'Social Capital in Building the Social Economy', in R. Pearce (ed.), *Social Enterprise in Anytown* (London: Calouste Gulbenkian Foundation, 2003).

28. S. Bridge and K. O'Neill, *Understanding Enterprise, Entrepreneurship and Small Business* (Basingstoke: Plagrave Macmillan, 4th edition 2013) pp. 277–279.

29. D. Halpern, *Social Capital* (Cambridge: Polity Press, 2005) p. 35.

30. S. Bridge, *Rethinking Enterprise Policy* (Basingstoke: Palgrave, 2010) pp. 187–188.

31. L. Pirolo and M. Presutti, 'The Impact of Social Capital on the Start-Ups' Performance Growth' in *Journal of Small Business Management*, Vol. 48 No. 2, 2010, pp. 197–227.

32. S. Bridge, B. Murthagh and K. O'Neill, *Understanding the Social Economy and the Third Sector* (Basingstoke: Palgrave Mcmillan, 2009) p. 84.

33. F. Delmar, 'The Psychology of the Entrepreneur', in S. Carter and D. Jones-Evans (eds), *Enterprise and Small Business* (London: Pearson Education, 2000) pp. 132–153.

34. S. Shane, *A General Theory of Entrepreneurship* (Cheltenham: Edward Elgar, 2003) pp. 2/3.

35. E. Chell, *The Entrepreneurial Personality: A Social Construction* (London: Routledge, 2008).

36. E. Chell, *The Entrepreneurial Personality: A Social Construction* (London: Routledge, 2008) pp. 82/3.

37. R. Peterson and R. Rondstadt, 'A Silent Strength: Entrepreneurial Know-Who', The 16th ESBS, efmd IMD Report (86/4) p. 11.

38. P. Graves, *Consumer.ology* (London: Nicholas Brealey Publishing, 2010) p. 29.

# Index

Accountants 2, 5(ill.1.1), 18, 23, 67–8, 71, 150
achievement motivation (NAch) 245
*Adapt* 142
affordable loss principle 46(ill.4.4), 219(ill.23.1)
*American Economic Review* 59
Amundsen 74
Apple 112

Banks 13 (ill.2.10, 200, 226
Banker/bank manager 18, 23, 67/8, 111, 137/8, 223,
Babson College 28(ill.3.1)
Baileys Irish Cream 110–11
basic skills 56
Baumol W. 151(ill.16.1), 240–1(ill.23.2)
*The Beermat Entrepreneur* 154(ill16.2)
behavioural economics 59, 62/3, 168(ill.18.1), 216–7
*A Better Mousetrap* 42(ill.4.1), 44
bird-in-hand principle 46(ill.4.4), 219(ill.23.1)
Blank S. 44(ill.4.3), 113–5(ill12.2)
Bourdieu P. 232
*Bowling Alone* 233–4, 236
Brain 177

left and right hemispheres 201–4, 210/11
Bridge, S. 5(ill.1.1), 15(fig.2.1), 85 (tab.18.2), 86 (fig.8.2), 239, 243, 244
Brooks D. 61(ill.5.2)
Burton (and Speke) 74
(business) consultants 2, 18, 23, 68, 71, 155
*Business Enterprise: Its Growth and Organisation* 19 (ill.2.2)
business plans Part 1 passim
  business plan hegemony 23, 29, 51, 69, 199
  business plan layout 15(fig.2.1), 17(tab.2.2)
(business) professional 18–19, 22–4, 27, 34, 39, 60, 67/8, 150, 187, 197 (ill.21.1), 222
business school(s) 18–19, 23, 68
business support agencies 4(ill.1.1), 23, 223
(business) trainers 18, 23,

Campbell C. 237
Cantillon R. 132
Caterpillar 21(ill.2.2)
Causation 45–7(ill.4.4), 99, 182–3, 217–221
Caution 24, 131, 187, 196, 221–3

Chell E. 247
clocks and clouds 60, 61–2(ill.5.2)
Coca-Cola 22, 109–10
Coleman J. S. 232, 236
Columbus C. 52–4(c.5.1), 54–6, 57–8(ill.5.1), 74, 92, 144, 194
*Columbus: His Enterprise* 55
company
 Community Interest Company 225
 company limited by guarantee 11(ill.1.4), 224
 company limited by shares 224
*Consumer.ology* 33(ill.3.3), 110, 135
conventional wisdom 39
cook(ing a meal) 99, 182–3
Cope J. 234
crazy quilt principle 47(ill.4.4), 220(ill.23.1)
'Customer Development' methodology 43(ill.4.3), 114(ill.12.2)

Department for International Development (DFID) 231
D-Day 35–6
Delmar F. 246
*Democracies in Flux* 236
Dewey T. 115
Digital 111
Donne J. 148
*Dragons' Den* 154(ill.16.2)

Earls M. 60, 62, 148, 229–30
Edison T. 79(ill.7.2)
Edwards, R. and Townsend, H. 19–21(ill.2.2)
effectuation 2, 44–50, 45–8(ill.4.4), 51–2, 65, 69, 97, 99, 121(ill.13.2), 138–9, 180–3, 196, 198, 202, 205, 208, 217–21
elevator pitch 153(ill.16.2), 248–9
embryo business 9, 49,
*The Entrepreneurial Personality* 247
explorers / exploring 2, 8(ill.1.3), 8–9, 48 (ill.4.4), 49–50, Chapter 5 *passim*, Chapter 6 *passim*, 72, Chapter 7 *passim*, 82, 90–3, 100(t.10.2), 107, 112, 115–8, 125–6, 126–7(ill.13.6), 128(ill13.7), 131, 133, 135, 136(ill.14.1), 139, 141–4, 148–9, 165–7, Chapter 20 *passim*, Chapter 21 *passim*, Chapter 22 *passim*
external funding 56, 197

factors of production 230
failure 24, 33(ill.3.3), 57, 77, 79–80(ill.7.2), 85, 91, 94(ill.9.1), 97, 100(tab.10.2), 115, 137, 139, 142, 144, 186, 196, 198, 208–10, 209(ill.22.1), 223,
financial capital 147–8, 157–8, 230–1, 234, 238

Franklin B. 168(ill.18.1),
Fukuyama F. 238

Galbraith J. K. 39, 59
getting started 57, 66, 78–9,
  Chapter 13 *passim*,
  185–6, 221, 223
Gladwell M. 235
goal(s) 7–8, 46–7(ill.4.4),
  55, 57, 66, 76,
  82(tab.8.1), 84–5,
  86(fig.8.2), 87(tab.8.3),
  92, 98(tab.10.1),
  100(tab.10.2), 182, 185,
  189(tab.20.1), 195, 205,
  212, 218, 220(ill.23.1)
  goal-realisation device 7,
  66, 81
Goss K. 236
Graves P. 33(ill3.3), 110,
  115, 135, 168(ill18.1),
  183

Halpern D. 239
Handy C. 208
Hanifan L. J. 231
Harford T. 142–3
*Heart, Smarts, Guts and Luck* 28(ill.3.1)
Herd 60, 148
hierarchy of needs
  83(fig.8.1)
Holywood Old School
  10–11(ill.1.4)
human capital 231, 233,
  236

IBM 111
intellectual capital 231
*International Small Business Journal* 234

Japan 53(c.5.1), 57–8(ill.5.1),
  74, 144, 194
jigsaw puzzle 46(ill.4.4),
  208

Kahneman D. 32(ill.3.3), 59
Kennedy W. 42–3(ill.4.2)
know-how 97, 101,
  156(tab.16.2), 230, 249
know-who 97,
  156(tab.16.2), 230,
  249–50

Lean Startup 42,
  43–4(ill.4.3),
  113–5(ill12.2)
*The Lean Startup* 115(ill12.2)
legal structures 223–6
Lehrer J. 61–2(ill.5.2)
lemonade principle
  47(ill.4.4), 219(ill.23.1)
Linn P. 168(ill.18.1)
locus of control 245

The Management Trinity
  160(ill17.1), 162(ill17.2),
map(s) 57–8(ill.5.1), 65,
  75, 115, 117(ill.12.3),
  136(ill.14.1), 167, 208
  route map(s) 135(ill.14.1)
market research 15(fig.2.1),
  22, 30, 33(ill.3.3),
  36, 45(ill.4.4), 89,
  Chapter 12 *passim*,
  135, 168(ill.18.1), 180,
  183–4, 186–7, 205,
  209–11, 222–3, 250–2
Marvin L. 76
Maslow A. H. 83(fig.8.1),
  84

Masters J. 85
McGilchrist I. 131, 176, 201–4, 212
mentor(s) 38(ill.3.4), 68, 114(ill.12.2), 151(ill.16.1), 152, 153–4(ill.16.2), 161, 162(ill.17.2), 189((tab.20.1),
Mintzberg H. 29, 121–3, 132, 174–5
Morgan, General Sir Frederick 36

need for autonomy 245
Newton I. 61(ill.5.2),
Nobel Prize for Economics 59

Ogilvy D. 110
O'Neill, K. 5(ill.1.1), 15(fig.2.1),
*Outliers* 235

*Paint Your Wagon* 76
Penrose, E 20–1(ill.2.2), 29–30, 40, 49
Peterson R. 156(tab.16.2), 230, 249
Philip II of Spain 142
physical capital 231, 236, 241
pilot-in-the-plane principle 47(ill.4.4), 121(ill.13.2), 138, 220(ill.23.1)
Pirolo L. and Presutti M. 240
Popper Sir Karl 60, 61–2(ill.5.2)
Prince's Trust 38(ill.3.4), 154(ill.16.2)

*The Prince's Trust Guide to Starting Your Own Business* 38(ill.3.4)
professional (*see business professional*)
prospectors 74, 141
Putnam R. 232–7

radar 85
Read S. *et al* 134(tab.14.1), 137, 219–20(ill.23.1)
Ready-Fire-Aim 120–1(ill.13.2)
*Rethinking Enterprise Policy* 84(tab.8.2)
Ries E. 43–4(ill.4.3), 113–4(ill.12.2)
*The Rise and Fall of Strategic Planning* 175
risk 17, 55–6, 73, 77, 89–90, 92–3, 109, 129(ill.13.7), 132–3, 134(ill.14.1), 136–8, 181, 184, 187, 189(tab.20.1), 198, 210, 223, 228, 245, 250
risk-taking propensity 245
rock-climbing and the rock-climbers' approach 124, 125(ill.13.5), 223
Rondstadt R 156(tab.16.2), 230, 249
Roseto. 235–7
Rumsfeld D. 133

sales forecasts 15(fig.2.1), 17, 30, 33(ill.3.3), 184, 191(tab.20.2), 200, 251–2

INDEX 275

Sarasvathy S.  45–8(ill.4.4), 89–90, 99, 116, 134(tab.14.1), 138, 143, 182–3, 186, 198, 217–20.
scientific theory  44–8(ill.4.3), 104(ill.11.1)
Scott  74
seesaw  176
self-actualisation  83(fig.8.1), 83–4
sense of adventure  49, 55
Shane S.  143, 246
Silicon Valley  44(ill.4.3), 113(ill.12.2)
Sirolli E.  160(ill.17.1), 162(ill.17.2)
Small and Medium Sized Enterprise (SME)  227
Smith A.  231
Smith G.  236
social capital  63, 66, 77, 79, Chapter 16 *passim*, 162, 166, 205, 229–42, 250
social enterprises  8(ill.1.3), 87, 242–4
society's rules  151(ill.16.1), 240–1(ill.23.2)
*So what? who cares? why you?*  42–3(ill.4.2), 42–4

Speke and Burton  74,
Stalinist Russia  142
Starbucks  143
startup syllabus  18, 23–4, 37(ill.3.4)
strategic planning  15(fig.2.1), 16(tab.2.1), 30, 121, 175–6, 220(ill.23.1)
Swiss Army knife  199

*The Theory of the Growth of the Firm*  20(ill.2.2)
third sector  243–4
Tjan A. T. *et al*  28(ill.3.1)
Traits  136, 218, 243, 244–8
*Trust*  237

Udacity  115(ill.12.2)
*The Undercover Economist*  142
(the) unexpected  35–6, 77, 87(tab.8.3), 131, 135, 136((ill.14.1), 138–9, 141, 209(ill.22.1), 210–11, 219(ill.23.1), 221

working capital  231

The manufacturer's authorised representative in the EU is Springer Nature Customer Service Centre GmbH, Europaplatz 3, 69115 Heidelberg, Germany. If you have any concerns regarding our products, please contact ProductSafety@springernature.com

Printed and bound by CPI Group (UK) Ltd, Croydon, CR0 4YY
23/03/2026
02076734-0012